COMMON
WISDOM

COMMON
WISDOM

COMMON
WISDOM

8 Scientific Elements of a Meaningful Life

LAURA GABAYAN, MD, MS

Published by:
Redwood Publishing, LLC
www.redwooddigitalpublishing.com
Orange County, California

ISBN: 978-1-956470-99-4 (hardcover)
ISBN: 978-1-956470-91-8 (paperback)
ISBN: 978-1-956470-92-5 (e-book)
Library of Congress Control Number: 2024903196

Interior Design:
Jose Pepito

Cover Design:
Michelle Manley, Graphique Designs

*To my kind husband Shervin and
sweet children: Jacob, Gabrielle,
Michael, and Sarah. Thank you
for always supporting me.*

*Of course, a big thank you to the
sixty wise interviewees, who were the
reason I was able to write this book.*

CONTENTS

AUTHOR'S NOTE

I t has forever been part of my culture, as a Persian Kurd, to believe that hard work and persistence lead to success. Included in that was the assumption that I have complete control of all aspects of my life. I became a physician because I liked the academic challenge and have always had a desire to help people. I specifically pursued emergency medicine (EM) for two reasons: I felt like EM was pure medicine that treated people based on immediate need, and it also taught me how to manage every situation life would throw my way—from life or death to the mundane. I then pursued scientific research because I enjoyed the challenge of discovery and inquiry and believed I could contribute more to medicine in this way and have a greater impact on the world.

Yet, little did I know that the universe had a different plan for me. In 2013, I was diagnosed with an autoimmune condition. Like most people in my situation, I was initially shocked, sad, and angry. I then came to view my illness as a challenge I would overcome. As I was erroneously diagnosed and received the wrong treatment, that challenge became more difficult and my condition worsened. By 2015, walking had become more difficult, and I could only see patients while seated on a rolling chair. I began to question my days as a clinician. That is when I started to think outside the box.

I was determined to overcome this condition by any modality possible. I realized that while traditional Western medicine had *some* answers, they were not enough. I pursued other styles of healing and learned to think unconventionally. I slowly realized that this devastating condition was a gift that helped me question the meaning of my own life. This is also when I started paying attention to those who have more depth in their approach to life and those who see life with more meaning: the wise.

While attaining wisdom is a life's purpose for many people, the teachings and commentary about wisdom are anecdotal. As a scientist, I needed more objectivity, so I created The Wisdom Research Project. My goal: to understand wisdom from a scientific perspective. I developed a process in which I personally interviewed sixty adults, ages fifty to seventy-nine, in an attempt to determine what wisdom is and how we attain it. Each person graciously shared their thoughts about wisdom, which I then analyzed using my research skills.

The findings of the project are fascinating. Wisdom is a state of being—a mindset. From a librarian who lives in the smallest home in her neighborhood to a CEO of many companies, I dis-

I discovered wisdom was not related to accomplishments or wealth but is a passion and love of life that results in meaning and depth.

covered several commonalities in their approach to life, which I analyze and discuss in the following chapters. It was clear from my research that having wisdom is not related to accomplishments or wealth. It is a passion and love of life that results in meaning and depth. The findings of this project are both priceless and timeless.

Enjoy!

ABOUT THE WISDOM
RESEARCH PROJECT

For years, I was interested in the wisdom of others. Although I knew I wanted to study wisdom, I did not know how. So, I began reading the scientific literature about wisdom in various journals. I learned that wisdom was either philosophical (what is found through scientific studies and published mainly in geriatrics, psychology, and sociology journals) or spiritual (religious). Life wisdom was the ultimate goal for many people and was regarded as a state of ultimate mastery of being. It is a universal desire to make sense of the world we live in—we all want it.

The scientific literature gave me a foundation for how to design my project and determine who could participate. Multiple studies found that wisdom had an inverse U relationship with age, and although gaining wisdom was the benefit of aging, the very old started to lose their wisdom as they became more set in their ways and less flexible in their thinking. I also learned that wisdom was not associated with gender, political affiliation, or race. Wisdom was, however, associated with the culture or country a person was from. Despite the published tests, wisdom could not be tested or

Wisdom can't be tested or measured with a scale; rather, a person is declared "wise" simply through another person's opinion.

measured with a scale. The gold standard for declaring a person "wise" was another person's opinion.

Even though I didn't yet know everything about wisdom, I knew how to design a research project. So, I started there. I created an online scheduling platform and obtained an internet subscription for video conferencing. The scheduled video conferencing allowed for face-to-face interviews with each person for a minimum of fifteen minutes. While still virtual, this gave me and the interviewee time to form a more personal and intimate connection with each other versus just speaking over the phone, which I felt was too impersonal for such an important project. I hired a marketing specialist and research assistant ("The Team"), who were essential to keeping the project moving forward. We met for one to two hours twice a week online to discuss the progress of the study. We created a website and began discussing the project with people we knew, whether it was clergy, co-workers, friends, or family. We also posted the project on internet sites such as Nextdoor and Reddit, as well as other social media platforms.

Over a seven-month span (October 2022 to April 2023), I interviewed sixty candidates whom I called my "interviewees." Weekly, I met between two and five interviewees, asking ten open-ended questions (as shown below) over a minimum of fifteen minutes. Each interviewee was invited to nominate other people they knew who they considered wise, allowing the project to grow and continue. Most interviews were recorded.

Here are the ten open-ended questions each interviewee was asked:

1. Why were you nominated for this study?
2. In one minute, describe yourself, your life, and your life experiences.

3. Was there a life experience/obstacle that served as an impactful learning experience?

4. What ideals/mantra do you live by?

5. When you think of yourself today, what values motivate you?

6. In a typical day, what is very important to your way of living/happiness? What can you not live without?

7. Gratitude has been found to be associated with wisdom. Was there an event that made you more grateful?

8. How do you deal with the difficulties of life?

9. What words of wisdom do you have for the younger generation?

10. How did you gain your wisdom?

People in the research project were between fifty and seventy-nine years of age and had to be nominated as wise by someone twenty-five or older. Self-nominations and nominations of parents were not allowed. Based on prior literature, we defined "wise" as 1) making good decisions and/or 2) giving sound advice. There was no incentive for nominating someone for the project or taking part in the interview. The person participating in the project would be kept up-to-date regarding the progress of the project and was promised to receive a copy of this book once published.

Upon completion of the interview, the team reviewed the recorded interview and discussed the theme or themes that described the interviewee. (Note that in qualitative research, the results of your data are to identify "themes," but these can be just as easily described as a "trait." Throughout the book, we use the words "theme" and "trait" interchangeably.) Themes are a way to convert stories into data. We saw many themes repeating themselves throughout the various interviews, and we realized that being "wise" is often comprised of more than one component. Several lists of themes and subthemes were circulated among the team, and in an iterative way, themes were expanded and collapsed until a final list emerged. After poring through the interviews, my team composed the list of common themes as follows:

1. **Resilience**—the ability to weather through difficulties.

2. **Kindness**—being friendly, generous, and thinking of others.

3. **Positivity**—the practice of being optimistic in life.

4. **Spirituality**—a belief that there is something greater than being human.

5. **Humility**—to be humble and modest.

6. **Tolerance**—having sympathy for those around us and for other beliefs or practices that differ from our own.

7. **Creativity**—the ability to think about problems differently or to look at scenarios from a new perspective.

8. **Curiosity**—a desire to learn and an interest in those around you.

Each interviewee was found to have at least two themes. A majority had at least five themes, and only one person had all eight.

Throughout this book, we will take a closer look at each element. There are also some stories or comments made by the interviewees. Some of the names of the interviewees have been changed for confidentiality purposes.

CHAPTER 1

WHAT IS WISDOM?

The journey of a thousand miles begins with one step.
—Lao Tzu

What is wisdom? Can it be scientifically defined? For millennia, people have defined wisdom in a variety of ways, yet all seem to rely on an idea that can be phrased as "I know it when I see it." Can something so important be left to intuition, or can wisdom actually be quantified? Answering this question became the premise of The Wisdom Research Project and the basis for this book. The goal of this study was to scientifically determine if wisdom is what in Latin would be called *sui generis* ("of its own kind" or "in a class by itself") or if wisdom was a combination of different elements. In other words, is the purpose of life to attain wisdom, or do we use wisdom for the purpose of attempting to understand the meaning of life? Or both?

The Wisdom Research Project used scientific methods to determine that wisdom is a combination of eight primary elements that work together. These elements, which will be discussed at length in the following chapters, are resilience, kindness, positivity, spirituality, humility, tolerance, creativity, and curiosity. Many of these elements may appear obvious, and others may be surprising, but after reading this book, you should be able to determine which of these elements you have mastered and which of these elements you can improve upon in a practical way.

Unfortunately, in today's culture, it seems that wisdom has taken a backseat to superficiality. Wealth, glamour, and self-promotion have all become qualities admired and valued by the masses. Many people have developed an obsession with attaining power and a need to increase followers on social media. On top of that, many use the anonymity of the internet to express hateful thoughts and question the wisdom of the day. These traits are not what wisdom is all about—in fact, it is the exact opposite. This is why working to understand wisdom is so important. As Lao Tzu said, "Great acts are made up of small deeds." Unfortunately, it seems that is a lesson embraced in the past. It is my hope that with this book, we can place more focus on the traits of wisdom that I mentioned earlier and work to build a stronger, more supportive society and connection with one another.

From the time of the inventions of the wheel and writing, and throughout many different cultures, wisdom has been considered a most valuable quality, earned through knowledge and experience over many years. About 2,500 years ago, Confucius taught, "By three methods we may learn wisdom: First, by reflection, which is noblest; second, by imitation, which is easiest; and third by experience, which is the bitterest." The ancient Greeks acknowledged the importance of wisdom by

> *Wisdom has been considered a most valuable quality, no matter which culture or religion we study. It is said to be earned through knowledge and experience over many years.*

imbuing it in their goddess Athena. The ancient Greek philosopher Socrates believed that wisdom is directly tied to humility. He stated, "The only true wisdom is in knowing you know nothing." Socrates taught Plato, who was quoted as saying, "A library of wisdom is more precious than all wealth, and all things that are desirable cannot be compared to it."

Aristotle and his teacher, Plato, cared deeply about wisdom and argued about its definition. According to Plato, wisdom required knowledge and its manifestation was to have good judgment. Aristotle, by contrast, felt that wisdom was not aimed at actions but more connected with understanding the abstract and that "Knowing yourself is the beginning of all wisdom."

Hinduism, thought to be the oldest known religion in the world, is estimated to have originated around 4,000 years ago (between 2300 and 1500 BC). Some may argue that since it lacks a prophet, Hinduism is more of a way to live than a religion, and the Hindu belief is non-exclusive and accepts all other faiths and religious paths. Hinduism believes in the acquisition of knowledge and posits that when insight is added to knowledge, it results in wisdom. The Bhagavad Gita (a

700-verse Hindu scripture) says of Hinduism, "Those who possess this wisdom have equal regard for all." This wisdom is also thought to result in a respect for all living beings, whether a cow, dog, or human.

Daoism (sometimes spelled Taoism)—which has been found to date back to the sixth century BC (about 2,600 years ago)—believes in the will of the divine and the wisdom of the universe. It believes one should think lightly of oneself and deeply of the world. Daoist teachings come from shamans or healers who incorporate the message of the mystical into their daily lives. Daoism believes in simplicity, patience, and compassion, and that every living being is guided by an energy or *chi* and should live in harmony with the universe. The universe is constantly changing and flowing, and we must yield to it rather than forcefully impose our beliefs on it. If we do, we are truly able to observe and better understand all that is around us.

Buddhism has also been traced back to the same time period and is similar to Daoism, yet there are some clear differences. Buddhism had a founder—the Buddha, or "enlightened one"—who is at the core of its teachings of wisdom itself. While knowledge is important to

Buddhism, it is not the foundation. In Buddhism, wisdom is realizing or perceiving the true nature of reality and being open to change while having courage, patience, and flexibility. Buddhism believes that suffering and experiences shape one's reality and that the path to enlightenment is achieved through morality, meditation, and wisdom.

This brief overview of religions and philosophies shows us that there is a commonality of thought about wisdom. They each recognize that wisdom describes a depth of character and inner "truth," but how do we perceive wisdom today? The *Oxford Dictionary* describes wisdom as the "capacity of judging rightly in matters relating to life and conduct; soundness of judgment in the choice of means and ends." The Wisdom Research Project discovered the components of this ability.

The Wisdom Research Project dissected wisdom and identified its many elements. While the eight elements we discovered appear to be distinct, they are all related. The following chapters offer an in-depth view of these elements and can help readers identify their own strengths and weaknesses regarding wisdom. They will also help us determine if the purpose of life is to attain wisdom or if we use wisdom for the purpose of attempting to understand the meaning of life.

CHAPTER 2

RESILIENCE

The way I see it, if you want the rainbow,
you gotta put up with the rain.
—Dolly Parton

R esilience was the most common element associated with wisdom. It makes sense. When we
think about people who have encountered a difficult life challenge and resolved it with grace, we tend
to regard them with special admiration. We become
intrigued by how that person managed to not only survive the obstacle but thrive. We realize that, because of
that experience, they likely now have a different perspective on life. They have turned a potentially negative
experience into a positive learning opportunity, making

them wiser. The more of these life challenges they overcome, the wiser they seem to be. As Oprah Winfrey once noted, they turned their "wounds into wisdom."

Although we mentally compare the types of obstacles and their gravity, all obstacles are difficult, regardless of how we quantify them. What may seem like a minor challenge to us may be a major life-altering event to someone else. Whether it be a strained relationship, health crisis, or loss of a loved one, wise people view life's challenges as lessons. They don't view themselves as victims but rather as students—here to learn lessons that would have otherwise never been learned. In essence, they believe they *needed* that obstacle. It helped further shape who they are and built their character. The bigger the obstacle, the bigger the lesson, and as is often said, "The harder you fall, the higher you bounce." While this "bounce" cannot be physically measured, the idea is that the bigger the obstacle, the greater the reward (in most cases, more wisdom).

The *Oxford Dictionary* defines resilience as "the capacity to withstand or to recover quickly from difficulties; toughness." A resilient person has "tough skin" and can withstand anything, and this recovery from obstacles builds on itself. It is like a "mental muscle" because the more it is used, the easier it becomes to bounce back. It's similar to physical exercise and building stamina. If you've ever worked out to get back into shape, you likely remember that those first couple of weeks were brutal; usually, each day brought you sore muscles you didn't even know you had, making even getting out of a chair a cause for celebration. However, after you've been working out for a month, you barely break a sweat. It's the same with our life challenges. This is why those who have had more experiences—usually older individuals— have a better ability to cope with adversity. They've been "working out" longer. The younger generation is less resilient simply because they have not yet experienced as many difficult situations. They're just beginning to "work out." Another example is the experience of having children. It's very difficult to raise children, but people often feel like once they overcome the "hump" of having the first one, it is not as difficult with the rest. They have learned that not every bump or bruise will lead to a hospital visit. The worry over the first child's pacifier falling on the floor is no longer there with subsequent children. They have become wise regarding parenthood and tend to not sweat the small stuff.

Resilience is a way of being. It is a mindset that you are not a victim but a warrior. Life is not always fair and is full of obstacles that have to be overcome. Helen Keller said, "Although the world is full of suffering, it is also full of the overcoming of it." In many ways, it is accepting that notion that puts us at peace and lets us be prepared to fight. It's not that we are on high alert every moment of our lives; it is that we know life will throw us obstacles, but we are prepared to take them head-on and are confident we will overcome them.

> Resilience is about realizing that life won't always be fair and will be full of obstacles that need to be overcome. Being resilient means creating a mindset that you are not a victim but a warrior and that you will overcome these challenges and come out on the other side.

Inner resilience first starts with how you feel about yourself. It's the knowledge that you are strong, and you are capable of overcoming anything that comes your way. It's a sense of self-confidence and integrity. It is knowing that what you stand for matters for yourself and others. By having self-respect, you ensure that others have respect for you as well. All these things combined contribute to an inner strength that's necessary for resilience. At the end of the day, we all want to be loved and respected. Being respected by others will lead to more feelings of self-confidence, and this, in turn, will lead to a greater sense of self-worth. It's a self-perpetuating cycle.

Remember the famous saying, "What doesn't kill you makes you stronger"? An obstacle serves as a lesson, resulting in a more resilient and wiser you. In fact, after each obstacle, you become more and more equipped to say, "I can do it," to the next obstacle. This inner confidence feeds how you interact with the outside world. Resilience also instills in you a sense of gratitude for the challenge. You welcome the obstacle and think, *Bring it on*. Over time, you view every obstacle as a challenge to be overcome, secure in the knowledge that you will come out the other end with even more knowledge, experience, and confidence in yourself.

This inner resilience also means you have the integrity to take full responsibility for your thoughts and actions. Someone with inner resilience can take the emotional "hit" if reprimanded by a superior when things go wrong and accept responsibility for failure. More importantly, that person can learn from it and become wiser because of it.

An obstacle can also serve as an awakening or major life-changing experience. Maybe you or someone you know has gone through a horrible life event and completely changed their perspective and life as a result. This is often referred to as a "spiritual awakening." Deepak Chopra said, "Awakening is not changing who you are, but discarding who you are not." Dr. Joe Dispenza is a chiropractor focusing on the mind-body connection. He is an international speaker and writer whose message is that every person has the ability to heal. He attributes his life and message to an accident at age twenty-four. While cycling, he was hit by a truck. This resulted in him breaking six vertebrae and being told he would never walk again. He spent hours daily using his chiropractic skills to reconstruct his vertebrae in his mind and attributes this to his becoming fully recovered in eleven weeks and walking out of the hospital. He believes that is how powerful the mind is. By working to tune your mind into what you want your body to do, you can create your own reality.

Your resilience can have an impact on others as well. History is full of examples of people who embody resilience and have changed the world. Ludwig van Beethoven was a German composer and pianist who composed what many consider to be some of the most brilliant classical music, all while losing his hearing. Abraham Lincoln grew up very poor, yet he taught himself law and eventually became a highly revered US president. Walt Disney loved to draw to escape his repressive, cruel father and, despite many stumbling blocks, was successful in his creation of the iconic animated character Mickey Mouse. Rosa Parks, the African American woman who refused to give up her seat to a white person, helped launch the movement to stop segregation in the American South. Today, we may think that refusing to move from a bus seat is a simple thing to do, but in the fifties, this one act was difficult and responsible for giving the civil rights movement the push it needed. The resilience of others can really be inspirational. It can motivate us and give us hope. The examples above show that ordinary human beings can accomplish extraordinary things, changing the world, and so can we.

In spiritual terms, a way to view an obstacle is that it is there to develop your soul. In many ways, the fact that it is there is a sign that the divine feels you can master it and it won't break you but will make you stronger. In a surprising way, the obstacle is a gift. Have you met people who seem to have the perfect life? Interestingly, many seem shallow and lack depth of character. Every difficult situation for them is accompanied by much drama and is a big deal. They also seldom give good advice. If you were to need a friend by your side while going through a difficulty, that friend who seems to "have it all" is not who you'd want. That person lacks perspective. You would seek someone who's more "real" and down-to-earth. Someone who understands that bad things happen and has a more positive perspective about things.

One of my interviewees, Bob, is a gay dad. He went through many obstacles to become a father. He not only dealt with the ability to adopt his kids (and had to involve the US Congress in the process) but also had to deal with many judgments he faced throughout the experience. He fought long and hard to achieve his goal of becoming a parent, and he never gave up. Now more than ever, he feels that one should be proud of who they are and stand up for themselves.

Another way to attain resilience is to believe that things do not happen *to* you but *for* you. When things seem to be going wrong and your life seems to be encountering great turbulence, think of the bigger picture. Realizing that these experiences help us become stronger, smarter, more resilient, and thus wiser changes these experiences into something much more powerful and transformative. It's easy to ask *Why?* or *Why me?* Instead, try asking *Why not me?* That question, along with the confidence that you can handle it, will lead to greater resilience.

Believing that things do not happen to you but for you is key to developing resilience. Instead of getting frustrated, convinced that everything is going wrong, people with resilience will see what's happening as a learning lesson. Something that will make them stronger.

Clara, another Wisdom Research Project interviewee, is currently a life and love coach. She was born in jail. She was also part of the foster care system because of horrific abuse from her mother. Yet she has never let her past define her. In many ways, it awakened her. It gave her a realization that the scars have allowed her to be who she is today. She believes that "Everything is perfect" and that things will always work out as they are supposed to. She has used the obstacles in her life to increase her resilience and wisdom.

We've identified many of the qualities that make up resilience, but how do we build resilience? The interviewees were asked how they dealt with difficulties, and all had similar responses. They felt that there were four key steps in building resilience:

1. Acceptance.
2. Gratitude.
3. Tackle it head-on.
4. Release worry.

Part of acceptance is having an emotional moment and then releasing the emotion. Holding a grudge, for example, doesn't really impact the person you're resenting, but it does impact you by keeping you stuck in that emotion—and also in that moment in time. Only by releasing the feelings of being wronged and hurt can you move forward. Another element of acceptance is taking a step back and giving yourself time to think things through and perhaps sleeping on it. We have all been blindsided by something that has thrown us off balance, like being unexpectedly laid off at work, for example. Taking some time to think about your options will help you make sound decisions about your future. Obstacles are managed better with a clear mind.

The second step is gratitude for the challenge, which is manifested by a simple "thank you." By giving thanks, you acknowledge the challenge and also that it will be resolved. Gratitude for the universe presenting us with the opportunity to learn and grow is a critical step in developing resilience.

The third step is how you address the difficulty. By approaching it head-on, you are taking control of it and not letting it control you. Ignoring the problem never solves the problem. Only by confronting the problem directly can a problem be solved.

Finally, the fourth step is recognizing that worrying about it will not change the end result. It will not impact the outcome in the least. Worrying about a problem only creates a higher level of anxiety. Have you noticed that your worries never come true? You can think of all the reasons why your son may not come home, how the dental procedure can go wrong, or how you can lose something important. Yet, how often do those concerns ever happen? Not very often. So it's best to not spend the energy worrying about something that probably won't happen. As Tom Petty sang, "Most things I worry about never happen anyway."

In spiritual terms, letting go of concern for the outcome is to "surrender." It's an unusual term in that, in practical terms, it means to "give up," but in spiritual terms, it means the opposite. It means to accept the reality of things, do what you can to the best of your ability, and then step aside to let the universe take over. A spiritual surrender means you are not focused on or worried about the outcome. It is a difficult concept to understand, and it will take time to grasp. Think about how when it rains, you do everything to prepare for it, and then you accept that it's raining and do not worry about the outcome; you are grateful that the vegetation is receiving the water it needs.

The steps of resilience discussed above are easier to accomplish with support. When encountering an obstacle, talk to others and confide in loved ones. "Two heads are better than one" is a well-known sentiment because it's true. Many studies have concluded that social interactions lead to greater happiness, lower risks of dementia, and a greater sense of safety, belonging, and security. So, too, will other things that bring you happiness. Surround yourself with pleasant pictures and enjoyable music. Meditate and envision overcoming the challenge. Imagine times when you have been carefree and have overcome similar obstacles. Be compassionate toward yourself and give yourself the support you deserve.

Acceptance is very important to Sissy, another interviewee. She has survived the death of not one but two husbands. These two experiences would send many people into a tailspin they might not pull out of. For Sissy, after each death, she accepted her new reality and was able to continue to move forward in her personal and professional lives. Of course, she grieved, but she knew that her life had to go on if she was to find happiness and inner peace once again. Her belief that we have to accept both what we can and cannot control allowed her to work through her grief and thrive. It also allowed her to help others by writing a book exploring how life does go on for those who have suffered a loss.

A common sentiment regarding resiliency among our interviewees is the idea that to overcome obstacles, one has to be "fiercely flexible." They believe this trait leads to an ability to adapt to circumstances and challenges so they can better tailor a response to the difficulty. Think about an intense windstorm: The rigid tree breaks while the flexible bush survives.

> Remember to be "fiercely flexible." This will allow you to adapt to any challenge as well as find creative ways to solve your problem.

Instead of being emotional and inflexible when faced with a challenge, recognize that there are other ways to solve the problem.

The interviewees who were resilient were fearless and driven, and they expressed emotional control. There are many ways to be fearless. Cliff diving from great heights takes fearlessness. For many, speaking in front of a large group of people requires fearlessness. First responders who run toward danger exhibit fearlessness. Accepting a new challenge takes fearlessness. It is a state of mind that reflects the belief that you have the ability to accomplish whatever is needed, regardless of your fears.

Scott, an interviewee who's a Presbyterian minister, teaches his congregation to "laugh often and fear not." This is based on several biblical principles. Fear is a natural concern of the unknown, yet it can be crippling if left unchecked. Living in fear will prevent you from living a happy life. It will prevent you from dreaming and, more importantly, acting on that dream, keeping you stuck in your current circumstances. On a physiological level, living in fear will elevate your cortisol levels, keeping you in a fight-or-flight mode where you're only focusing on survival. This will, in turn, hinder your imagination and ability to think creatively. It will impede your ability to live and enjoy life.

The interviewees also discussed the importance of "drive," of never giving up when faced with a life challenge. They felt that if you gave up, then you "gave up on life," and that was not an acceptable option. As Confucius said, "Our greatest glory is not in never falling, but in rising every time we fall." Mahatma Gandhi never gave up and used "ahimsa"—nonviolence—to bring a powerful empire to its knees in the service of freedom for the people of India. Regardless of the obstacles he faced and the negative encounters he experienced, he believed in the goodness of people. He often said, "You must not lose faith in humanity. Humanity is like an ocean; if a few drops of the ocean are dirty, the ocean does not become dirty."

Another element the interviewees discussed was their ability to control their emotions when confronted with an obstacle. They mentioned that younger individuals often lack this ability. Emotional control is a way to separate the emotions from the facts. While having emotions about a situation is cathartic, it does not help resolve the obstacle. The situation may be difficult, but difficult means it's manageable and possible.

Susan, another interviewee, lost her only child—her son—when he was sixteen years old. The death was earth-shattering and extremely difficult. Her life seemed to stop for several years. She then had the thought that, to honor his life and the positive impact he had on her life and others, she needed to accept that life must go on. This reawakened a sense of joy in her. She created a website in his name and went back to being "Mama Sue," the social butterfly she had always been. In everything she does, she believes that you should "find your joy." For her, joy has always meant bringing people together.

Resilience often leads to success in life. Another interviewee, Paul, the creator of the Adversity Quotient (AQ), author of numerous books about the AQ and who has helped build resilience in individuals in nearly 150 countries, recognized the importance of resilience when he was nineteen. There wasn't a specific life event that sparked his interest in resilience, but it was then that he started searching for the reasons why some people fail and others succeed. He has since done extensive research on the topic and has made it his life's work to measure and strengthen resilience in others.

💡 CHAPTER TAKEAWAYS:

- **Resilience is about seeing yourself as a warrior and <u>not</u> a victim.**
  Resilience is the ability to withstand difficulty and bounce back. It is an ability to view challenges in a different light and know that they are there to serve a purpose. It's having hope that anything is achievable. It is a view that

an obstacle is not there to "break" you but to "make" you.

- **Resilience is the cornerstone of wisdom.**
  It shows depth of character and perspective, and the more you practice resilience, the further this depth of character develops. Having resilience starts with one's outlook and builds with practice. As difficult as it might be to practice, try to put emotions aside and encounter obstacles directly. Know that living in fear will take away your strength to persevere.

- **Your resilience can have a profound impact on those around you.**
  Your reaction to your own challenges can offer hope and inspiration to those around you. It can provide people the confidence to be able to weather their own storms.

THINGS TO ASK YOURSELF:

This next section is interactive. To use it, start with the first question. Fill in the date you are answering the prompt and write down your thoughts. Your answers will change with time. At a later date, when you come back to the chapter, re-read it and answer the questions. Look back at what you wrote previously and reflect on how much you've changed. What have you learned? Have you gained additional wisdom and insights as you've grown?

- What does resilience mean to you?

    Date: _____

    Answer: _____

    _____

    _____

    _____

    Date: _____

    Answer: _____

    _____

    _____

    _____

- How quickly are you able to adapt to a challenging situation?

Date: _____
Answer: _____

_____
_____
_____

Date: _____
Answer: _____

_____
_____
_____

- How often have you been emotionally "thrown" by unexpected news in the last year? How did you handle it?

Date: _____
Answer: _____

_____
_____
_____

Date: _____

Answer: _____

_____

_____

_____

_____

- How do you react to a last-minute change in plans or appointments?

  Date: _____

  Answer: _____

  _____

  _____

  _____

  _____

  Date: _____

  Answer: _____

  _____

  _____

  _____

  _____

- What is one thing you can do to improve your resilience?

  Date: _____
  Answer: _____

  _____

  _____

  _____

  _____

  Date: _____
  Answer: _____

  _____

  _____

  _____

  _____

KINDNESS

*We make a living by what we get, but
we make a life by what we give.*
—Sir Winston Churchill

ccording to our research, kindness was considered the second most important element of wisdom. It was a surprising finding but understandable. Kindness is highly valued in all cultures and is a trait we all gravitate toward. Jack Kornfield wrote *Buddha's Little Instruction Book*, in which he adapted the ancient Buddha teachings for the modern world. In it, he wrote this about being kind: "Words have the power to both destroy and heal. When words are both true and kind, they can change our world." Being kind has far-reaching implications and shows that you respect others. We all deserve respect. Kindness means different things to different cultures, and we found that it can take on infinite forms.

Kindness is expressed in many different ways, both physically and emotionally. As Mark Twain once said, "Kindness is the language which the deaf can hear and the blind can see." Opening the door for a father trying to wrangle a couple of toddlers or driving a neighbor to a medical appointment are examples of physical kindness. Physically doing something to help another person is kindness in its most observable form. Paying someone an unexpected compliment about the cookies they baked or letting a friend vent about their frustrating day are examples of emotional kindness.

One thing is certain: Kindness can make something difficult or painful

While it may take some time to develop the trait of kindness, eventually it will feel like second nature. Kindness needs to come from your heart and not have any strings attached to it. It should feel like very little effort on your end, but it makes a big impact on those around you.

much less so—for both the giver and the receiver. When given from the heart, kindness is one element of wisdom that makes a big impact with very little effort. That is the key regarding kindness. It must be genuine and heartfelt and not based on convention or obligation. Mahatma Gandhi is quoted as saying, "The simplest acts of kindness are by far more powerful than a thousand heads bowing in prayer." Being kind is rewarding and increases feelings of self-worth.

The *Oxford Dictionary* defines kindness as "being friendly, generous, and considerate." As previously explained, it's a simple concept, not burdensome to do, yet it has long-reaching impacts. Being kind does not negate one's effectiveness or success in getting their point across. You can be firm but still be kind. For example, if a co-worker asks you to complete a task she's been assigned, rather than saying, "Sorry, I can't help you" and walking away, you could show kindness by saying, "I wish I could help, but I'm in a time crunch myself. Have you spoken to our supervisor about this yet? He may be able to help you find a solution or give you an extension." Those few extra words can have a big impact. In fact, being kind often results in better results because it communicates an air of reason and calmness, not anger.

Being kind to others is important, but it begins with another form of kindness that the interviewees feel is equally significant. Many participants strongly believe that kindness starts with being kind to one's self. At the core of this is self-love and a lack of hypercritical self-judgment. Self-care has been a big buzzword for many years now, but it's an important piece of kindness. Whether it's sitting in your car on your lunch break to give yourself some peace and quiet, getting a monthly pedicure, taking solo hikes on weekends, or even just not checking work emails after dinner, self-care is the first step in practicing kindness. In fact, the interviewees often agreed that taking time out of your day to care for yourself was part of what made you a better person. Some scheduled that time and looked forward to that time. It was the most important time of the day or week. For some people, acknowledging the importance of this time may be challenging. Some people may view self-care as selfish or self-indulgent. We have a natural negativity bias and tend to focus on our "failures" or disappointments instead of seeing something positive about ourselves or our situation. For example, we may remember having dressed inappropriately for an event, having accidentally said something inappropriate in a public situation, or getting a poor grade, but we seem to easily forget how we held the elevator for an older person on the way to that event or how hard we worked for that grade (and that it was an improvement over the last grade).

Being kind to ourselves makes it easier to be kind to others and makes a lasting impression on the receiver of that kindness. Your cup is full, so you can bring happiness to others. People will long remember the feeling they had when someone was kind to them. Abraham Lincoln recognized the importance of kindness when he said, "Kindness is the only service that will stand the storm of life and not wash out. It will wear well and will be remembered long after the prism of politeness or the complexion of courtesy has faded away."

For some people, it's more difficult to be kind, particularly if they weren't raised in a supportive and kind environment. The good news is that kindness can be learned, regardless of age and circumstance. It may require a little more work, but it is not impossible.

Repetition is the key. The more you are kind to yourself and others, the easier it gets to integrate kindness into your everyday life. It's a habit that needs to be developed. Just like brushing your teeth, being kind will become easier (and maybe even something you begin to do without much effort) once you develop it as a habit. It just becomes part of your everyday routine.

Oftentimes, when you are in an upsetting situation and are angry, it is difficult to be kind. Yet, it's more important than ever not to overreact. Nothing should be said or done in an emotional state. Take deep breaths and give yourself fifteen minutes to calm down and think about what you need to say or do. By stepping back for a few minutes, your perspective will change. Instead of letting your emotions speak, let all communication come from *you*, not your emotions. As author Greg Clarke said, "To talk without thinking is to shoot without aiming." Pause before speaking. Know that words can have unintended consequences; therefore, you should be very careful with what you say. This is a common thought the interviewees shared: They firmly believe that one should "think before you speak." As the Bible says, "The tongue is a small thing, but what enormous damage it can do."

Kindness is a quality that many appreciate in others. Those who are kind often avoid those who aren't. They find it difficult to interact with inconsiderate, antagonistic, or energy-draining people. As Ralph Waldo Emerson said, "The only reward of virtue is virtue; the only way to have a friend is to be one." At the core of kindness is a deep love and respect for humanity. It is displayed by being gentle and having empathy, grace, honesty, and transparency. All types of relationships flourish when based on kindness and respect. There is a reason that the phrase "Do unto others as you would have them do unto you" is considered the Golden Rule.

A highly successful scientist, Tomas, another of our interviewees, feels that the philosophy of treating others with kindness was what helped him transition more easily in his move to the United States from Czechoslovakia. He was born and raised in Czechoslovakia and then moved to America prior to attending college. Despite living under completely different governments and in different cultures, he realized that people, regardless of where they originate, want similar things: to be loved,

respected, and surrounded by kindness. This understanding helped him relate to people in the United States
and also served him well while building his life as a scientist. He also feels that it is through kindness that he
is able to resolve conflicts. He believes in treating others
with "fairness and acts of selflessness." Being in charge
of a large research group, each with its different agendas
and needs, has made him aware of the vital importance
of focusing on the needs of everyone in helping solve
complex problems. His focus is always to ensure that the
solution leaves all parties satisfied.

Another interviewee, Cathy, has served in many
different capacities, including as a nun, social worker,
and life coach; she feels the greatest help one can give
another is to "be the eye of the storm" when they're
going through a difficult time. The idea is to be calm
when someone is stressed. You've probably heard the
phrase, "Be kind, for everyone you meet is fighting a
hard battle." While some attribute this to Plato, it's now
widely regarded as having been penned by Ian McLaren,
a Scottish author (although phrased slightly differently
as "Be pitiful, for every man is fighting a hard battle").

In an unusual way, kindness is selfish in that it leads to a greater reward than expected. This is a case of the whole being greater than the sum of its parts. The psychological effect on the person being kind is easy to understand; it makes them feel happy and content to be kind. The psychological effects on the one receiving kindness can encompass feelings of truly being heard, feeling respected, feeling gratitude, and other positive emotions.

Kindness can instantly turn someone's bad day into a good day just by another's thoughtful act. Mother Teresa said, "Spread love everywhere you go. Let no one ever come to you without leaving happier." The feeling that people get when they interact with you is what will stay with them. Not the details. Another aspect of a greater reward simply by being kind is seen in problem-solving. How many times have you noticed that people being kind tend to get

Being kind to somebody can stay with the recipient longer than you think. They may not remember the details of your kindness after some time, but they will remember how they felt when they interacted with you.

their lost luggage returned quicker, their appliances repaired faster, and impossible appointments scheduled with more ease?

It is also important to note that kindness toward others is easy when they're kind to you. It's much more challenging when they are not. That being said, as mentioned earlier, being kind—regardless of the circumstances—helps you as much or more than it does the other person. It is a sign of wisdom to take the high road and approach the unkind person with compassion. Martin Luther King Jr. said, "Let no man pull you so low as to hate him." Kindness is the way to counteract the negative thoughts and behaviors we cannot help but encounter in modern life—and may even help the unkind person change their way of thinking, feeling, and behaving. Unkind people are not pleasant to be around, but simply being kind to them can have a positive impact on them, as well as you.

If the interaction goes beyond someone being unkind and turns into a conflict, then kindness can play a large role in its resolution. In order to resolve any conflict, it first needs to be de-escalated. Nothing gets resolved in anger. So, it's important to maintain the perspective that you are on the same team, even if you appear to be at odds with someone. You both want to resolve the conflict. Parents may argue about the type of discipline for a child, but they both realize they have their child's best interest at heart. In the end, they both want a resolution, which usually ends in a compromise, but it *will* be resolved. Stephen, an interviewee who's written a book about conflict resolution, agrees with the statements above and feels that kindness is a key factor in conflict resolution. He believes kindness transforms anger and revenge into calmness and reason. He also feels that a large part of resolving a conflict is being considerate and trying to understand the other person's perspective.

Being kind to others is especially critical when one is in a position of power and can require extra effort and consideration when interacting with subordinates. This applies to obvious situations, such as a boss/employee or teacher/student relationship, as well as other situations, such as the dynamic between a high-ranking leader in an organization and a newcomer. Think of how impactful it was when someone was kind to you on your first day of a new job or at school.

Kindness isn't just a social construct; it also has spiritual implications. Three of the world's largest religions (Christianity, Judaism, and Islam) advocate for thoughts and acts of kindness. A foundation of Buddhist teaching is loving-kindness, the idea that through loving others and being kind to those around you, you in turn benefit. They all teach that kindness constitutes giving freely of your attention, time, and money and not expecting anything in return.

Richard, another interviewee, is an attorney who left his law practice to study and work as a chaplain after deciding he wanted a more fulfilling role, one that would bring more meaning to his life. He wanted to *be* rather than *do*. Rather than doing and completing legal paperwork and billing hours, Richard wanted to *be* the pillar of support and strength a person needed during a time of difficulty. Now that he's a chaplain to hospice patients, he is extremely satisfied with his life and is able to spread more kindness to those in need. It reminds him daily of how he hoped his mother was treated in her final days. He feels that by being kind, he receives more than he gives.

We have discussed *what* kindness is and how it is viewed in different cultures. Now, we will discuss *how* to practice kindness. Being kind starts with simple acts. First and foremost, be kind to yourself by starting a daily practice that can take as much or as little time as you have available. It can be a simple ritual of putting your hands on your chest as an act of acknowledging yourself, giving yourself praise, looking in the mirror and smiling, taking at least three deep breaths, or meditating. Regardless of how you feel about yourself, know that you are special and your presence is important to at least one person around you. This ritual needs to be simple, and it needs to acknowledge yourself. You know yourself better than anyone, so make sure that what you choose to do for your daily practice fits with your temperament and your schedule. As is the case with physical exercise, the more complicated your routine, the less likely you will be able to continue it for the long term. Regardless of what you choose, it's important to know that the habit of giving yourself that time every day will change who you are in profound ways.

Once you've mastered your daily practice for yourself, you can focus on being kind to others. When interacting with another person, acknowledge their presence with a smile and eye contact. Consider an embrace. Express kindness through simple gestures such as writing a note, text, or email. Work to catch yourself if you start to say something critical to another person; ask yourself if what you're about to say is necessary or unkind. If you find that you are judging, choose silence instead. Remember the saying, "If you don't have anything nice to say, don't say anything at all." Words to live by. When you need to be critical, and sometimes it is necessary, the most effective (and kind) way of going about this is to begin with a compliment, then state

While being kind to others is important, remember that kindness needs to begin within yourself. Being kind to yourself (practicing self-care, engaging in positive self-talk, cheering yourself on, loving yourself) will give you the confidence to easily spread kindness to others.

the criticism, and then finish with another compliment. Think of this as a kindness sandwich with the critical comments in the middle. This is a less intense and more positive way to deliver a message, leaving the person feeling like they've had a positive exchange and not personally attacked. This will result in greater motivation and the desire to do better in the future. People have an innate desire to please. Notice that people are much more accommodating when you ask for their help rather than when you demand it.

In addition, using specific details when showing your appreciation for someone else is more impactful. People like to feel acknowledged with specifics. Be precise when pointing out how someone did something positive. It shows them that you noticed and appreciate them. These acknowledgments should originate with "I" statements, such as, "I appreciate how you anticipated our client's needs in that presentation." Using specifics lets the other person know that you truly do value what they've done for you.

Another important component of kindness is empathy, or the ability to understand and share the feelings of others. It shows that you care, are open to new ideas, and are willing to consider another perspective (theirs!). This helps you be more considerate by coming from a position of understanding and not judgment. You can almost make a game of it by trying to figure out why someone thinks or behaves a certain way and then approaching them and asking (in a kind, neutral way) about their thought process. You may be surprised how much you will learn about people, the world, and yourself by doing this.

Transform this from an intellectual exercise into actual practice by incorporating more random acts of kindness into your daily life. Buy the person behind you in line their coffee. Bring your neighbor their newspaper or mail. Give a candy bar and a sincere "Thank you" to the delivery man. You will feel good—and so will they.

One of our interviewees, Frank, lost his sister several years ago to cancer, and watching her deteriorate (as well as how she was treated by other people) solidified his appreciation for kindness. During his interview, he shared his experience of seeing a strong, active mother wither and become thin, emaciated, and so weak she could barely stand. The random kind gesture by a nurse or the thoughtful act of a caretaker stuck with him. Because of this experience, empathy has become the quality he values most in a person. He volunteers weekly at a hospice care facility that provides end-of-life services to individuals with less than six months to live. This opportunity allows him to be kind to those in need. Taking his empathy a step further, he's also become a vegetarian because he does not want to harm animals.

When asked why someone was nominated for the study, a common response was that, in addition to living a life of purpose and being "grounded in wisdom," the nominees help others whenever they can. Helping people regularly was viewed as a noteworthy quality. Giving is an important aspect of the lives of the interviewees, who believe that we all share this earth with others and it's our responsibility to help when we're able.

Rabbi Adam K., an interviewee, was bullied in school as a child. He was a good student and slightly chubby, and as a result, he was taunted and teased every day. This experience left a lasting impression on him. A large portion of who he is today and how he manages his congregation is a reflection of his experience as a child. Now that he is influential to others and has the opportunity to deliver sermons regularly, he goes out of his way to make sure he emphasizes the significance of kindness and fairness to his congregation. He also lives his life believing that "You are owed very little by the world—you should live as if you owe." He feels that we should always give more than we receive.

An interesting element and subtheme of kindness that the participants discussed was forgiveness. Forgiveness was viewed as a powerful tool and a foundation of healing. Debby, who went through a bitter divorce, now sees the truth in the maxim, "Forgiveness helps the forgiver more than the one forgiven." To forgive is not about forgetting what happened or about coming to understand why it happened, but instead about recognizing that the other person made a mistake that was hurtful—and that regardless of the size of a mistake, it was a mistake. Through forgiveness, we release that hurt and begin the healing process, which allows us to move forward in a healthier way.

Forgiveness is all about you, the person who was hurt. It's about no longer letting the hurtful incident impact you in a long-term, significant way. Bill, a theater producer, director, and writer who's recently encountered acts of hate in his neighborhood in New York, feels that forgiving allows him to live his life on his terms. During his interview, he shared that instead of giving in to the hate, he chooses to be kind and compassionate and help those in need. If he saw that a neighbor who was hateful needed help, he would offer to help. He uses forgiveness almost as a shield against negativity.

The saying "Forgive and forget" means that you decide not to be angry about the incident and not let the memory of it affect you. You "forget" the negative feeling it created but not the offense itself. Doing this helps you move on.

Forgiveness does not mean you're okay with what happened. Elyce, another interviewee, feels that it is forgiveness that allows her to have the rich life she now lives. This, despite having endured several horrible crises and health challenges, including assault from her ex-husband, as well as the loss of a child and grandchild. Forgiveness is the only way she was able to overcome the many traumatic experiences she encountered. Forgiveness gave her hope that her life would improve, and it was the first step she took to help her move forward. She's now a successful spiritual life coach, is married to a wonderful man, helped open a church, and truly loves her life. She feels that forgiveness is an act of kindness toward yourself. Forgiveness means that you are no longer a victim impacted negatively by what happened. A kind person sees the bigger picture and does not take things personally.

They also see the good in others. A kind person is secure about who they are. Incorporating kindness into one's life is not easy, but it is simple.

Pain and hurt happen to everyone. That is just a fact of life. Those who cannot forgive go through life weighed down with anger and resentment. Not forgiving results in more pain for the person who was hurt. Those who forgive have a lightness about them, unburdened by the weight and darkness of negativity. By forgiving, we take back our power and accept that we both experienced and survived the pain. In a way, kindness is a secret weapon and forgiveness is at its base.

💡 CHAPTER TAKEAWAYS:

- **Being kind starts with being kind to yourself.** If your own cup is full with the kindness you are giving yourself, you will be much more able to bring that same attitude toward those around you. People remember how they felt when being around you, and if you are speaking down to yourself or criticizing yourself, others will feel that. Kindness is an important part of wisdom, and it starts with you.

- **Kindness needs to be from the heart.**

  Being kind should not be done to get something out of people or for your own benefit. It should be genuine and heartfelt—recipients of your kindness should not be made to feel that they "owe you." Remember this even when you are in a difficult situation. At some point, you will find yourself feeling upset at someone, but you can still be kind as you work through your emotions. Remember to take a few breaths, calm down, and try to understand where that person is coming from. Then respond.

- **Forgiveness can be a key to unlocking kindness.**

  Forgiveness is a way to allow yourself to heal from traumatic or upsetting situations. When practiced, it can help you to release all the pain and hurt that you felt and move forward in your life in a healthy way. Instead of giving in to the hate or the hurt, you can choose to fight it through kindness.

THINGS TO ASK YOURSELF:

- What is the kindest thing someone has ever done for you?

  Date: _____

  Answer: _____

  _____

  _____

  _____

  Date: _____

  Answer: _____

  _____

  _____

  _____

  _____

- What is the kindest thing you have done for someone else anonymously?

  Date: _____

  Answer: _____

  _____

_____

_____

_____

Date: _____

Answer: _____

_____

_____

_____

- Can you remember an incident where you failed
  to show kindness and now regret it?

Date: _____

Answer: _____

_____

_____

_____

Date: _____

Answer: _____

_____

_____

_____

_____

• What is one thing you can do to show yourself
  kindness?

  Date: _____

  Answer: _____

  _____

  _____

  _____

  Date: _____

  Answer: _____

  _____

  _____

  _____

  _____

CHAPTER 4

POSITIVITY

Count your age by friends, not years.
Count your life by smiles, not tears.
—John Lennon

P ositivity was the third most prevalent element in our study. This is understandable because positivity is a strong indicator of how someone approaches life, obstacles, and opportunities. If you think about which friends and family members you prefer being around, most likely it's those who have a more positive disposition. After all, who wants to hang out with a grumpy, negative person who drains the energy of any room they enter? Curmudgeons are fun to watch on TV but not so much in real life.

We currently live in an age with more gizmos and gadgets designed to enhance our lives and provide a greater level of comfort than at any other time in history. On paper, this should provide a greater sense of happiness and a more positive outlook on life, yet with all of our modern comforts, finding truly positive people is oftentimes more difficult than expected. The rise in social media apps, which people use to highlight only the "fun" parts of their lives, causes those following to self-doubt their own happiness and, in turn, makes them less and less positive about their own lives. It's more important than ever to learn the importance of developing a positive mindset as well as understanding how to maintain that throughout life's challenges.

People with a positive outlook typically believe that they have complete control of their thoughts and feelings and that positivity is their choice. Being positive also reflects a sense of optimism, calm, and hope.

The *Oxford Dictionary* defines positivity as "constructiveness, optimism, or confidence." A constructive person sees a situation as an opportunity to better their life. Circumstances may appear grim, but a positive person will somehow change it around so that it becomes a positive experience. Helen Keller said, "Optimism is the faith that leads to achievement. Nothing can be done without hope and confidence." Confidence is knowing that you can do anything and believing in yourself. It's not *if* we will encounter an obstacle, but *when*. Realizing that things could always be worse also contributes to a sense of optimism and positivity.

You can almost physically *see* when people know with certainty that they like themselves and who they are. They exude positivity. There's almost a Mona Lisa smile on their face, a sense of confidence in their stride. Loving yourself is important to attain wisdom because it allows you to be open to learning. You may not be a naturally positive person and may not have been born with a positive disposition, but

Positivity is a state of mind—not a state of your physical world.

you can learn to be. It simply takes practice. It doesn't come from wealth, family, or material goods. These external factors temporarily make you happy but do not last. This is why it seldom works to tell yourself that you'd be happier if you got that raise, lived in a bigger house, or lost weight. As Lynn, one of our interviewees, said, "Happiness is an inside job." Positivity is a state of mind—not a state of your physical world.

In a similar light, positive people tend to not sweat the small stuff. Have you met people who are perfectionists and obsess over their appearance, spend ten minutes writing and rewriting an email, or are upset because they find a stain on their jeans? These types of people often set unattainable goals and are disappointed when they fail; more often than not, they *will* fail because they are sweating the small stuff and ignoring the more important world around them. There are bigger problems in the world and greater difficulties that people overcome than a perfect appearance. A significant number of people across the globe can't afford designer jeans; some can't even put on a pair of jeans because they're disabled. When you realize that things can be worse, then you don't let little things get to you.

Another important element of staying positive is not having expectations, both of others and situations. When you have expectations of others, you set yourself up for possible disappointment, which makes staying positive more difficult. We can't control what others say, do, or think, but we can control our own thoughts and actions. Most times, recognizing that is enough to help us stay in a positive state of mind.

To be clear, expectations are slightly different than setting goals for ourselves and having a desire to achieve them. Goals give us a challenge to meet and drive us forward; expectations are often preconceived notions of a desired outcome and open us up to disappointment, as previously mentioned. Having a goal of getting a promotion drives us to work harder; expecting to get a promotion can lead us to negative emotions should we not get it. Consider a similar situation for a high school student applying to college. A personal goal is to work hard in preparation for college, but an expectation is for that hard work to get the student accepted into the desired college. That admission may not happen.

The same is true regarding other situations. Having an expectation of the outcome of a situation or an event can only lead to disappointment. You cannot control the outcome. For example, if you're responsible for holding a fundraiser and you do your best, you still may not achieve your expected goals. Even if the event is fun for the attendees and serves the purpose of generating media attention and bringing people together, it may not raise the funds you expected. You can't be disappointed because you gave it your best and the event accomplished many other goals.

Surrounding yourself with other positive people is very important for your own emotional state. Think about who you are attracted to. You probably gravitate toward the person with the smile, the one who's happy and optimistic. As a result, you feel the same. Their demeanor affects yours. Like yawning, positivity is contagious. You feel compassionate and hopeful when you are around these types of people. That is why the old adage, "Choose your friends wisely," is advice to live by. It's more important to have a small number of positive friends than a large number of friends with varying positivity. It's quality over quantity. Someone once told me, "Happiness is like jam. You can't spread even a little without getting some on yourself."

Practically speaking, being a positive person can impact your chances of earning a leadership position. While some experience may be necessary, a leader would much rather hire a person who they see as "constructive, optimistic, and confident" rather than one who is not. They know through experience that positive employees will be resourceful and hard-working, both key elements of success. More than that: Subordinates can be inspired to greater, more creative levels of effort if they have positive managers and leaders. Another practical result of being positive is that you become more engaged in your surroundings and your own life experiences, leading you closer to greater wisdom. Negative people tend to want to be left alone ("Get off my lawn!"), and thus miss out on life's learning experiences. Positive people like being around other people and being an active participant in their lives.

Helping others be more positive can be as simple as being supportive of a friend having a bad day. Reminding them that "Sadness is not forever," as Fred Rogers said, can put a smile on their face and help them through the difficulty. You are not minimizing their concerns but instead are helping them find the silver lining. Melanie shared that she believes you should sprinkle positivity in someone else's life every day and "Be magical, remain magical, be the wand." You can serve as the instrument that instills positivity in another person.

In a spiritual sense, positivity is rooted in a feeling that things will work out and that everything happens for a reason. It's also a recognition that we are not alone.

There is a higher power greater than ourselves that wants us to benefit from the experience. "Benefit" is not always what we think it is. What we perceive to be a favorable outcome may not be beneficial for us in the long run. We are humans who cannot always grasp the bigger spiritual journey we are on, so we may not understand why bad things happen to good

> Positivity is rooted in a feeling that things will work out and that everything happens for a reason. It's also a recognition that we are not alone.

people. We can't always understand why a child dies or a kind person gets cancer, but it's the belief in a higher power that can reveal a positive reason behind something that, at first glance, seems truly awful.

Have you noticed that many of the most successful people have encountered a "setback" that subsequently re-shaped their life for the better? This is the universe working *for* you. Oprah Winfrey was fired from a job in Baltimore as an evening news reporter and eventually relocated to Chicago, where she took a show from last place in the ratings to one of the highest-rated television talk shows in Chicago. What happened next? *The Oprah*

Winfrey Show. Albert Einstein was unable to get a job for two years after he earned his graduate degree and finally settled on working at a patent office, which gave him the time to write four landmark papers that subsequently changed the course of physics and the world.

Lynette, an interviewee who used to work in advertising and marketing, was not feeling well one day. In her interview, she recalled how she was taken to the hospital and discovered she had a ruptured colon. She had to have immediate surgery and remained in the hospital for three weeks. During this time, she was grateful to be taken care of and to be the recipient of love and support. The experience led her to start journaling and addressing four intentions every day: 1) Acceptance, 2) Affection, 3) Appreciation, 4) Attention. Journaling has been a source of strength and positivity in her life ever since. As difficult as the situation was emotionally and physically, it gave her much in return.

Being positive starts with a plan, a realization that you deserve to go through life being happy, regardless of your circumstances or situation. As we discussed in the Kindness chapter, start small. Start by having a single positive thought and doing one thing for yourself that makes you happy each day. Start by putting up pictures that bring a smile. Consider setting an alarm as a reminder to listen to a favorite song or to just take a deep breath. Make pursuing joy a priority. Even if it's for one minute, make positivity the foundation of your day. Read something that makes you happy. If you have a stressful life, you'll first want to pursue calm before joy. Regardless, the good feelings you get will cause you to want to do more to create positive emotions.

Positivity also requires that sometimes you need to pause for perspective. Revel in the realization that there's only one you. You are more important than whatever situation you encounter. Don't be so hard on yourself and stop pushing yourself. Remember that we are all doing our best—and especially that our best is relative, not absolute. Our best is a combination of our experiences and our current situation. We are in an age that measures productivity and résumé-building. Yet, people forget the big picture. A good rule of thumb is to think about whether the situation you're facing will be important in five years. If it won't, then let it go. Don't waste your energy on something that will have little or no impact on your own "big picture."

Have self-compassion and prioritize yourself. This starts with acknowledging your self-worth and creating a plan. It also starts with practicing saying "no." It might seem odd to be discussing both positivity and saying "no," but you can only be there for others if you're there for yourself first. This sometimes means saying "no" to things that will drain you instead of fulfilling you. Think of the emergency advice given to airplane passengers: Secure your own oxygen mask before helping others. Or consider the analogy about the state of one's "bucket." It's only when your bucket is full that you can be your best self. Being positive often requires you to attend to yourself first. You cannot give what you do not have.

Larry, who is committed to coaching and creating shows as part of *The Larry Show*, instills wisdom in adults over the age of sixty in his work. He refuses to even use words that have an air of negativity. When asked how he deals with difficulties in life, he said his first step is to catch himself going down the rabbit hole of negativity. Then, he changes the word "difficult" to a positive word like "learning experience." Using negative words is what he grew up with and now refuses to entertain. During his interview, he explained that he always says to himself, "I will not stay in the weeds; I will go to the mountaintop."

Eduardo, a former attorney, incorporates positivity into his daily life. Throughout his interview, he referred to himself as a "monkey" and laughed often. He feels that play is very important to his state of being and takes it to the "very limit of responsibility." He believes that "God is never happier than when he sees his children at play." In his marriage, he incorporates excitement and spice so that it's never boring. He has a zeal and love for life that is insatiable.

Consider saying a simple but powerful affirmation to yourself several times a day. The power of positive thinking is profound. Do not use negative terms in the affirmation. For example, say, "I am strong" instead of "I am not weak." Your brain will only register the term "weak" and not the word "not." "I am" statements are very powerful. Initially, you may not believe the affirmation, but soon you will. Say the affirmation silently or out loud and say it while overcoming an obstacle or while doing nothing significant. John Lennon felt that the mind was very powerful and incorporated these thoughts into his music. He believed that regardless of the difficulty, "Every day in every way, it's getting better and better."

Also consider doing a daily visualization. Visualize yourself doing what you want to be doing. Your brain won't know the difference between what is and is not real. There have been numerous instances where a person used their mind to "practice" a sport and became just as successful at the sport as the person who physically practiced. This can apply to every part of your life. For example, if you are having difficulty walking and you like the beach, visualize yourself running on the beach. Don't remind yourself of the prior limitation; visualize yourself running as if it's something you're used to doing. The visualization should be detailed and include an emotion. A way to include detail is to include at least three senses. What do you smell at the beach? Do you feel the rays of the sun on your skin? What do you hear? Truly feel the emotion of how running on the beach feels. Another type of visualization is to imagine that what you want has already happened. Visualize having gotten that raise, having given a successful presentation, or having a productive and pleasant meeting. Consider incorporating both types of visualizations in your daily routine, one of an image that has already happened and one as if it is currently happening. For visualizations to be effective, they have to be practiced daily for a minimum of five minutes. A visualization taken seriously can have profound results.

The actions of your body can also impact your emotional state. Notice your posture. Simply holding your head up and sitting upright will elevate your mood. Catch yourself slouching and fix it. Smile as much as you are able. When you wake up in the morning, raise your arms to mimic a "V" and thank the universe for another day. Julie, another interviewee, feels like daily movement of her body is very important. When her kids were little, she was used to having a dance party daily, and she continues the dance party now that they're out of the house. She also engages in WOW yoga, which instills a sense of gratitude.

Gratitude, while a subtheme in many of the other elements of wisdom, is much more prevalent in the positivity trait we explored. Incorporating a small amount of gratitude into your life will lead to more thoughts of gratitude. Some people start with writing a gratitude journal. Others try a gratitude jar or reading inspirational quotes of gratitude daily. A simple internet search of "gratitude' will reveal innumerable ways to be grateful. If you write in a gratitude journal at night, you'll notice that you sleep better. If you wake up at night and want to go back to sleep, it's gratitude that can stop your "monkey brain" and your inopportune to-do list. Writing down grateful thoughts in the morning can change the mood of the day. Charlotte is a professor of psychology and feels that "striving should be rooted in gratitude." One should be grateful for the opportunity to succeed. While going through life, you will have to "dig through the dirt to find the treasure," but you will eventually encounter the light at the end of the tunnel.

Leah, an interviewee who is a professor of gerontology, also feels that gratitude is an essential part of her life and teaching. She has her graduate students keep a gratitude journal as part of their lesson plan and as part of their "required" material. In her interview, she shared that she believes that entitlement is an impediment to gratitude. She believes that "part of what it means to be human is to appreciate time and life on Earth." This appreciation is recognized through gratitude. When you see that everything in life is a gift, instead of expecting it, you are grateful.

Another major subtheme of positivity was humor. For many, humor is a way to cope with the stressors of life. If you encounter a serious situation, humor can be a valuable key to overcoming it. Humor doesn't mean you aren't taking the situation seriously; it means that you are trying to emotionally take a step back from the problem and gain some perspective in order to make the best decision possible. In the world of work, humor helps corporate executives and other leaders connect with their employees. It helps build bridges and trust. Maya Angelou once said, "Don't trust people who don't laugh. I don't." Humor makes us more human. For an employee, humor can instill a greater work ethic. A happy worker is much more productive, so when choosing a work environment, it's important to look for a culture that includes levity.

Many people feel that they don't have a sense of humor at all, but that's not true. Everyone has a sense of humor; it's just that for some people, it's still hiding under the bed, afraid to come out. There are many types of humor: irreverent, self-deprecating, joke-telling, story-telling, observational, ironic, absurdist, sarcastic, and many more. You might not be able to tell a "three people walk into a bar" type of joke, but maybe you can see the humor in forgetting your umbrella on a rainy day or recognize Murphy's Law in action. Take a few minutes to think about what makes you laugh, and you should be able to figure out which type(s) of humor best suits you. Humor is not just for fun; it also lowers stress hormones and increases immune cells and infection-fighting anti-bodies, and it can leave your muscles physically relaxed. So, the next time you're faced with something serious, see if you can find the humor in the situation. You'll feel much better and make better decisions if you do.

It's also important not to take yourself too seriously and to have a sense of humor about yourself as much as possible. Doing this will lighten any mood and will instantly make others feel more at ease with you. This doesn't mean that you're not serious about the situation or don't care about what's happening. It means that you're choosing to lighten the mood. For example, if you're going through a health crisis and are doing everything possible to feel better, at some point finding the humor in a terrible situation can help lighten the load.

As we just discussed, in addition to fighting stress, humor improves overall well-being and strengthens the immune system. Many people believe they've healed themselves of a chronic medical condition using laughter therapy. Even if you are not suffering from a chronic condition, you can incorporate laughter into your life. There are many funny video clips online that you can watch, or consider taking a laughter yoga class. If you've never seen it, check out the outtake video of the Carol Burnett sketch with Tim Conway telling his elephant story. If you think you don't have a sense of humor, this will prove you wrong.

David, an interviewee who grew up with two alcoholic parents and was on public assistance, noticed that laughter became a large part of his life and it helped deflect pain. In his interview, he shared that when he was diagnosed with cancer years ago, humor helped him get through the many treatments he had to endure. He's now retired and currently runs a nonprofit that creates games and cartoons that carry positive messages and provide humor for young audiences.

Scott, the Presbyterian minister we met in the Resilience chapter, wore a clown nose during part of his interview. It is humor that allows him to relate to his congregation and tackle difficult moments. It's humor that makes him an effective youth pastor. He also feels that gratitude is essential and feels that it's gratitude "that will get you to the other side of a difficult situation." When life is difficult, he said, "Find things to be grateful for." If you're showered with negative situations, it's only focusing on the positive that will help you get through it. Humor and gratitude are very important to him.

For many, humor serves as a secret weapon or a superpower, a way to connect with others while showing that you are paying attention. It can help bring levity to an otherwise stressful situation. In communication, it can lead to more productive ways of relaying a message. One of the wealthiest men in the world, Warren Buffett, used humor throughout his business meetings. It was his way of being approachable.

💡 CHAPTER TAKEAWAYS:

- **Positivity is a state of mind.**
  Positivity doesn't develop from wealth or material goods. Having a lot of money in your bank account may make you happy as soon as you see the money in there, but over time it won't contribute to the internal feeling of happiness and positivity. Only when you understand that you

alone have complete control of your thoughts and feelings, and those thoughts and feelings can be made into positive ones, will you truly embrace this key trait of wisdom. Being positive starts with a plan—a realization that you deserve to be happy, regardless of your situation.

- **Being positive allows you to become more engaged in your own life.**

  Think about it: When you're feeling down or negative, you likely don't want anybody around you. You might avoid your friends, call in sick to work, or ignore calls from your family. Positive people, on the other hand, want the exact opposite—they want to be around those they love, enjoy new experiences, and be active participants in the lives of their friends and family.

- **Being positive helps you live a healthier life.**

  Being positive is essential to navigating life with ease. As you encounter obstacles, it is positive thinking that will make the obstacles less difficult. If those obstacles surface again, you will likely feel more equipped to tackle them and maintain a positive outlook about the situation and the end result. Over time, this will reduce your stress and how you react to certain situations. You will begin to feel gratitude for everything that comes your way, whether it be good or not so good.

THINGS TO ASK YOURSELF:

• Are you a "glass half full" or "glass half empty" kind of person? Why do you think that is?

Date: _____

Answer: _____

_____

_____

_____

Date: _____

Answer: _____

_____

_____

_____

- When faced with a challenge, how do you use positivity to overcome that challenge?

  Date: _____

  Answer: _____

  _____

  _____

  _____

  Date: _____

  Answer: _____

  _____

  _____

  _____

- How do you feel when being around positive people? What about negative people?

  Date: _____

  Answer: _____

  _____

  _____

  _____

Date: _____

Answer: _____

_____

_____

_____

- What one area of being positive can you improve upon in your own life?

Date: _____

Answer: _____

_____

_____

_____

Date: _____

Answer: _____

_____

_____

_____

CHAPTER 5

SPIRITUALITY

*We are not human beings having a
spiritual experience; we are spiritual
beings having a human experience.*
—Pierre Teilhard de Chardin

S pirituality was the fourth element associated
with wisdom. This is, perhaps, unsurprising, as
spirituality has been an important component
of human existence for thousands of years. We know
this because archeologists have uncovered Egyptian hi-
eroglyphics with symbols that denote the spirit and soul
in connection with the people and reflect their belief in
the afterlife.

There are many theories about why spirituality has been so important to human societies. Some believe that thousands of years ago, survival depended on people working together, so creating some type of spirituality was a means of developing group cohesion and avoiding behavior that would weaken the group, such as selfishness. Others believe that spirituality was brought to us by emissaries sent from a creator. For Christians, it is Jesus. For Jews, it is Moses. For Muslims, it is Muhammad. Native Americans believe in Neolin and Tenskwatawa. Regardless of how it came about, spirituality has the potential to bring more meaning to many, if not all, aspects of life.

The spectrum of spirituality can vary from not believing in a higher power at all to believing that everything is influenced by a higher power. This higher power can be thought of in various ways and is referred to as the universe, the divine, the great spirit, or God. Regardless of the name, the idea is that it is someone or something existing beyond the physical world.

This spectrum of belief may also change with age. We often find that younger people seldom think about the future, but with age, they may start to question their existence, its meaning, and the presence of a higher power. This type of inquiry is not surprising, as it is most likely tied to the anticipation of mortality.

The *Oxford Dictionary* defines spirituality as "the quality of being concerned with the human spirit or soul as opposed to material or physical things." It is the search for something beyond the physical world, attempting to connect to our spirit or soul. It is knowing that we are more than a physical being and that it's this spirit or soul that connects us to the divine and breathes life into our bodies. The word "spirituality" comes from the Latin word *spiritus*, which means "spirit" or "breathing." The breath is what allows life to exist. The Buddha felt that the soul was an essential part of being human and said, "Just as a candle cannot burn without fire, men cannot live without a spiritual life." The physical and spiritual go hand in hand. This search for—and belief in—the connection between the physical and the spiritual is also the path to wisdom.

While some believe that spirituality and religion are interchangeable, others see them as two separate ideologies. They might have similar goals of understanding the divine and discerning our path to spiritual enlightenment but may go about it in very different ways. Religion is based on worship and beliefs and is often practiced with others who hold the same feelings for worship and beliefs. On the other hand, spirituality is more of an individual practice based on one's beliefs. Spirituality is more about inner understanding than it is about external worship. Obviously, pursuing either or both is a matter of personal choice. Either will, hopefully, move you closer to attaining wisdom and deciphering the meaning of life.

Spirituality helps us understand the difference between right and wrong and keeps us honest and altruistic, however it comes about, all for the greater good of mankind, all other life, and our planet. People behave more moralistically when they believe in karma, the idea that "What goes around, comes around." People are also more cognizant of their actions when they believe they're being watched and judged

Spirituality is the ability to see that there is more to life than you. It is understanding what is right and wrong; it keeps us honest; it helps us fight for the greater good of humans, all other lives, and our planet.

by a higher power. The notion that there is an omnipotent entity not only impacts how we behave in our daily lives but also how we relate to others and how we view our place in the universe.

A large number of interviewees described themselves as spiritual in some way. For some, it was not their primary focus, while others felt that this bigger entity guided everything in their life and that destiny was inescapable. For example, one person described having had a flight canceled and they felt that their trip was "just not meant to be." Believing there was a larger plan helped them readily accept this change.

Spirituality is also misunderstood by many; since they do not physically *see* a higher power, they may not believe it exists. Yet there are situations or "miracles" that happen that don't make scientific sense. These events can't be explained by nature and the natural world and, therefore, must be the result of the supernatural world. Think about when a person, despite all odds, survives a horrible accident. Or a person who is shot in the head, but the bullet misses the brain, like the example of Malala Yousafzai, who advocated for the rights of women under a repressive theocratic government and, as a result, was shot in the head by a Pakistani gunman and survived. Now twenty-six years old, she's a revered champion for women's rights and received the Nobel Peace Prize in 2014 for her work. Ask any of your friends or family members, and you will probably discover, with some prodding, that nearly all have had some type of unexplainable or metaphysical experience.

As mentioned earlier, the idea of spirituality varies for every person. Developing a sense of spirituality is a journey that requires inquiry and reflection. As Ralph Waldo Emerson said, "Make your own bible." Figure out what works for you and what doesn't. Expand your perspective and reality. God means different things to different people. Although Michelangelo depicted an image of an old man in the sky in his Sistine Chapel fresco, you can create your own image of God and question "the old man in the sky" impression. If the idea is that God is nonphysical, then how can it have physical characteristics? We apply a gender to God, but the spirit has no gender. John Lennon said, "I believe in God, but not as one thing, not as an old man in the sky. I believe that what people call God is something in all of us."

What if you were to look at the course of history? How could a higher power allow for the Holocaust, genocides, or mass persecutions? These are occurrences that many fail to understand and even consider unfathomable. All we can do when we think of these events is remind ourselves that we are mortal and can't always understand the metaphysical world; we realize that both good and evil exist in this world. It is important to note that without evil, there would be no appreciation of good. It's like having a vacation that lasts forever; eventually, it no longer feels special.

Some people come to spirituality because of a powerful life event. For example, Anne, an interviewee, did not believe in spirituality; she was an attorney with a Type A personality. Spirituality was a non-issue for her. Then, her son died at the age of six, but before he died, he would recite spiritual/religious texts that she had never introduced him to. Because of this extraordinary experience with her son, Anne is now more spiritual and incorporates a belief in a higher power into her spiritual thoughts. She admits she doesn't understand this higher power, but she acknowledges that it exists. Her extraordinary experience with her son changed her own concepts about spirituality.

As Anne demonstrates, the key to gaining a greater awareness regarding spirituality is to be open-minded and not avoid or dismiss what we don't see or understand. Take comfort in believing that there might be something bigger than you and appreciate the journey and inquiry in the search for truth. Albert Einstein said, "My religion consists of a humble admiration of the illimitable superior spirit who reveals himself in the slight details we are able to perceive with our frail and feeble mind." One of the greatest scientists of our time acknowledged his belief that there is something bigger than us. Attaining spirituality requires continuous curiosity to achieve spiritual growth.

Regardless of how spiritual you feel or how important being spiritual is to you, we all have a component of spirituality inside of us. This nonphysical part of us can't be explained or described, but it's what makes us human and differentiates us from a non-living object, like a computer or a car. It influences our relationships with others and gives us a "gut" instinct about other people. Why do you connect with some people and not others?

Why may one person give you a "bad" feeling when you really have not gotten to know them? There are feelings that go beyond our five senses.

Jody is a librarian and feels that her job is her "spiritual practice." It allows her to connect with others, help them, and be kind to them. She stated in her interview that she also has noticed that people often use a librarian as if the person is a therapist, revealing thoughts, feelings, and situations that aren't related to a book search. During each of her library shifts, she feels like she's serving a greater purpose and helping people in more profound ways. Her experience solidifies her belief that what we say and do and how we behave affects others.

Regardless of how you define being spiritual, it can be as simple as connecting with others. The sense of community and sharing a goal or purpose can bring people together, and this can have tremendous health benefits. Think of the Blue Zones. There are five of these regions across the globe (Okinawa Prefecture, Japan; Nuoro Province, Sardinia, Italy; the Nicoya Peninsula, Costa Rica; Ikaria, Greece; and Loma Linda, California) that have the highest number of centenarians ever recorded. The quality most common to the inhabitants of these regions is a sense of community and faith. These people outlive others because they share more meaning and purpose.

To become more spiritual, first, you have to be curious about it. *What is spirituality? Why are so many people searching for it? What does it mean for me, specifically?* Then, you have to see the need for it in your life. *How will being spiritual make my life better?* Next, be open to the possibility that it exists. Then, study it. Surround yourself with people who have more spiritual beliefs. Let those who have a better understanding of spirituality guide you. As the founder of the Blue Zones and au-

To become more spiritual, you have to first be curious about it. Then, you need to understand the need for it in your life. Next, be more open and accepting of the idea that it exists in some way. Lastly, you need to study it by surrounding yourself with people who do believe.

thor of the bestselling book *The Blue Zones: Lessons for Living Longer from the People Who've Lived the Longest*, Dan Buettner says, "The people you surround yourself with influence your behaviors."

Then, based on what you've learned, decide if spirituality will make your life better. If so, then act upon what you've learned by incorporating it into your life. And finally, continue the process of learning and incorporating spiritual thoughts and deeds into your life more and more each day. Engage in activities that will heighten your spiritual awareness, for example, meditation, yoga, or experiences in nature.

Isabella was in the corporate world, feeling empty because she lacked a life that was meaningful. She wanted to gain a greater understanding of the spiritual world. In her interview, she revealed that she quit her job and sought to have a "Moses experience." She spent a week alone in the Egyptian desert to better understand what Moses went through. Her only human interaction was with a person who brought her food and water once a day. She lived and slept on the sand, away from connections to the outside world. She had always felt that there was more to life than a single identity or job, and this experience helped shape her. Spiritual practice is now a large part of her life as she guides others as a spiritual life coach. She followed the progression discussed above and now incorporates spirituality into her daily life.

Tammy has a PhD in psychology, works as a therapist, and researches spirituality. She feels spirituality is an important part of her life and it brings her great meaning. It lets her feel that her mere presence is enough and she does not have to "publish or perish" to gain the love of the divine. Tammy does not feel pressure to perform because she sees the bigger picture. She has an inner peace because she sees that she is "enough," regardless of what she does. She feels that her spirituality is rooted in gratitude and feels that "Gratitude to God is transformational." Instead of questioning the existence of a higher power, she's grateful that something bigger exists and is watching over her. She realizes that she does not understand this higher power but has a sense of security that it is there.

An understanding of this higher power is recognizing that this entity is benevolent and loving. It is there to help you. Many times, this "help" is not always viewed positively. For example, think about a person who develops a disease. Initially, they feel a gamut of negative emotions like anger or disbelief, but as they go through this experience, they gain greater insight and perspective and undergo positive spiritual growth. They recognize that they now know things and do things very differently than during their pre-disease state, and they consider these changes to be a positive result of their experience. The condition was difficult, but it gave them a new perspective and a different worldview.

Yet a difficult situation can also result in mixed feelings toward God. The presence of a higher power or spirituality often comes into question when people have had to endure great difficulty. Have you met people who have had cancer or lost a loved one and, since then, no longer believe in God? They question how such a tragedy could occur and if God even exists. How could bad things happen to good people? Spirituality helps us accept that what happens in this world does not always make complete sense.

A subtheme of spirituality discussed by the interviewees was prayer. For many, prayer is not just an attempt to communicate with a higher power; it's an opportunity to express hope and optimism. It's "putting it out there" so that your prayers *can* be answered. As Mahatma Gandhi noted, "Prayer is not asking. It is a longing of the soul." Similar to journaling, it functions as a means of getting a thought out and creating an intention. It is healing and cathartic. The act of praying helps us focus our thoughts and release those thoughts into the universe without expecting a result.

When you engage in prayer initially, you may feel awkward. However, the more you engage in it, the easier prayer becomes, and it will soon become a comfort and bring peace and clarity. View it as an investment in your inner being. The time you spend in prayer need not be long. It's not one of those things that the longer you do it, the more likely it will work. One minute of prayer has the same impact as one hour of prayer. It should be deliberate and intentional. Remember the phrase, "Mean what you say and say what you mean"? Being open and honest is the key to prayer.

Lynette, the person we discussed in the Positivity chapter, prays every day. She does this not because she is religious but simply because she believes that there's something greater than herself. She calls this time "breakfast with God" and feels like it's her time to be grateful. She does not feel complete without doing this every day. The action of prayer makes her feel that there is a purpose to her life. Her prayers are meditative and include everything that's on her mind. She does not expect a result from the prayer. She does not do this because she wants something. The act itself is the point.

Another subtheme of spirituality was faith. There was an understanding that everything would work out and all obstacles had a purpose. Things "working out" does not necessarily mean what we might think. It's not necessarily the resolution of an illness or a positive outcome in a financial deal. Remember: Not having expectations about a specific outcome is a key aspect of openness in matters of faith. It is often beyond our comprehension, but the idea that it will "work out" is that the resolution will impact us positively in other ways. Faith is a belief that in the bigger scheme of things, everything will be okay.

Lynn has a son who developed chronic fatigue syndrome at age twelve. She has served as his continuous caretaker ever since his diagnosis. In her interview, she shared that despite it being emotionally difficult, she has learned to be more patient, resourceful, kind, and less ego-driven. Throughout his illness, she has always asked herself, *What is the more spiritual perspective to better understand why this is happening?* She has had faith that there is a bigger purpose to her suffering. She has also written a book about her journey and teaches a course on illness.

💡 CHAPTER TAKEAWAYS:

- **Spirituality brings meaning and depth to life.**
  There is a spectrum of spirituality that changes, grows, and develops with life experiences. Spirituality can vary for every person, but it helps people see a greater purpose to their existence. Everyone is spiritual to some degree and can incorporate it more into their life if they choose. Start out by practicing prayer or meditation— just a few minutes a day (or a week, if you want to start slower!).

- **Remember to approach spirituality with an openness and willingness to learn.**
  Get curious about it—*what is spirituality, and why are so many people searching for it?* Ask yourself what it could mean for you and how it could possibly make your life better. Then, find people who have similar beliefs and ask them questions. *Where did their spirituality come from? How did they develop a trust in the universe?* Try to learn

from those around you and emulate their thought patterns if you think it would benefit you.

- **Just because you don't *see* a higher power does not mean it does not exist.**
  Every single day, there are situations happening that are unbelievable, miraculous, and unexplainable through just science. You can create your own image of a higher power as well as your own "guidelines" for being spiritual—figure out what works for you and what doesn't.

THINGS TO ASK YOURSELF:

- Are you more of a religious person or a spiritual person? What is the difference between the two for you?

  Date: _____

  Answer: _____

  _____

  _____

  _____

Date: _____

Answer: _____

_____

_____

_____

_____

- Do you believe in something greater than yourself? How did you come to that realization (or
  not)?

Date: _____

Answer: _____

_____

_____

_____

_____

Date: _____

Answer: _____

_____

_____

_____

_____

• How do you connect with your spiritual side?

Date: _____

Answer: _____

_____

_____

_____

_____

Date: _____

Answer: _____

_____

_____

_____

_____

• What role does spirituality play in your day-to-day life?

Date: _____

Answer: _____

_____

_____

_____

Date: _____

Answer: _____

_____

_____

_____

_____

- How can you incorporate more spirituality into
  your life?

Date: _____

Answer: _____

_____

_____

_____

_____

Date: _____

Answer: _____

_____

_____

_____

_____

CHAPTER 6

HUMILITY

Humility is not thinking less of yourself,
but thinking of yourself less.
—C.S. Lewis

H umility was the fifth element in our study. It was not specifically discussed by the interviewees often, but it was observed that many had accomplished quite a lot in their lives yet chose to minimize their accomplishments. Instead, they discussed their accomplishments with humility and an openness that revealed their life's focus to be more on the eight elements of wisdom instead of what our society currently considers "success," such as money, power, and position. Through their discussions, they showed their ability to change and adapt to shifting circumstances, foregoing ego for the greater good.

Humility is a virtue that has been recognized as important throughout time. Lacking pride or an ego, a person of integrity and depth of character is not concerned with being considered "less than" compared to others but rather believes we are all equal. As far back as Confucius, humility was seen as a core human value. It's interesting to note that ancient Greek and Roman cultures actually *valued* a sort of self-aggrandizement, where it was considered common to "toot your own horn" regarding one's own accomplishments, believing that it was actually honorable to do so. The transition from self-aggrandizement to the concept of humility occurred with the dramatic crucifixion of Jesus. The Bible talks, often circumspectly, about the importance of humility, and these ideas about humility have grown and endured ever since. By being secure, confident, and strong, one is open to questions and other ideas. A humble person knows that "the more they know, the more they don't know," and therefore, regardless of their position in life, feels that it's important to listen and be receptive to learning more about ways to improve themselves or a given situation or circumstance.

The definition of humility is "a modest or low view of one's own importance." The term "humble" comes from the Latin word *humilitas*, which means "grounded" or "from the earth." Think about when you say that somebody seems "down to earth." You say this because you feel that person does not openly brag nor secretly condescend in their thoughts, words, or deeds. This does not mean that a humble individual has low self-esteem or confidence. It is the opposite. A humble person is so confident that they do not need to be elevated by others or receive external praise. It does not make them feel "big" to make others feel "small." They feel completely secure in themselves. Thomas Merton said, "Pride makes us artificial; humility makes us real." Think about this—does it make you feel good to make another feel bad? If not, you already have some humility within you.

With this confidence and security comes an understanding that there's no such thing as being the best at something; that there's always someone who has accomplished more, knows more, or has more wealth. This understanding leads to the ability to grow and develop more as a person and as a leader. Leaders who lead from a place of humility are often more successful. For example, the person in charge of a company that sells a product to the community realizes that it is crucial to hear from the employees because they have a closer relationship with their consumers and can provide valuable feedback regarding their wants and needs and how to serve them. Humility is what allows the boss to listen and really hear what the employees are saying, gaining critical insight into the customers and their business. In 2013, *The Economist* discussed humility and wrote, "If leadership has a secret sauce, it may well be humility. A humble boss understands that there are things he doesn't know. He listens."

Tom, an interviewee, is the CEO of five successful companies, and his style of leadership is always to lead from the bottom, to be a "servant leader" so that others are successful. When thinking of a pyramid of hierarchy in a company, he views himself as part of the base of the pyramid, not the tip at the top. He believes the CEO's job is to focus on the connection between the company and the stakeholders and customers, and the only way a CEO can do that is by being at the bottom of the pyramid. For Tom, the distinction between what he referred to as "staged humility" and true humility is really important. Staged humility is acting like getting attention does not matter, but it really does. True humility is not being concerned about receiving attention or recognition. A good example is an anonymous donor not wanting any mention of their generosity but giving solely for altruistic purposes.

One of the most important positive effects of humility is the ability to better connect with others, establishing deeper and more meaningful relationships founded on compassion, empathy, and equality—not superficiality and power. If you're a business leader like Tom, think about how much happier, more effective, and more productive your employees would be if you approached them from a position of humility rather than from a position of power. Realizing that you would not have a business without your

Having humility will likely help you to connect to others in a deeper, more meaningful way. Your relationships with others can be built on compassion, empathy, and equality rather than superficiality and bragging competitions.

employees would certainly change the interpersonal dynamics within a company. The same principles also apply to personal relationships.

Pride, the opposite of humility, can lead to many destructive acts. Individuals with too much pride can be narcissists and base all decisions on selfish desires. Fascists and dictators have excessive pride and thrive on feeling superior and unaccountable for their actions. It is this sense of power and entitlement that has dangerous consequences. Adolf Hitler suffered greatly from hubris, believing that his thoughts, opinions, and actions were superior. As a result, he caused unimaginable devastation and death. Saint Augustine once said, "It was pride that changed angels into devils; it is humility that makes men angels."

Unlike pride, humility allows for personal growth and helps us continue to move forward in our lives. It allows us to learn from our past and present and focus on the future, keeping us from becoming rigid in our thinking and stuck in the past. Humility is a major component in keeping us working to better ourselves and continue learning, and that includes learning from other people's experiences so we don't have to go through the slow process of experiencing something on our own. Learning from others almost acts as a "time jump" because you can learn from someone else's particular life experience in a matter of minutes rather than take months or years to go through it yourself, but this is a choice you must make. Building a boat by trial and error could take you years to successfully figure out, but by asking the advice of someone who's already built a boat, it may now only take you a matter of months, saving you time, energy, and money. Make the decision and the effort to talk to people who've done something you have not. If you're recently married, talk to a couple who've been married for twenty-five years and learn what it takes to create a successful marriage. If you've just joined an organization, talk to the director and other co-workers and learn more about how they successfully achieve their goals. If you're a first-time parent, talk to a parent who has older kids. Listening and learning from others can only happen from a place of humility.

Humility is also related to Emotional Intelligence. Emotional Intelligence, simply put, is the ability to manage both your own emotions and understand the emotions of people around you. There are five key elements to Emotional Intelligence: self-awareness, self-regulation, motivation, empathy, and social skills. Those five key elements truly can only exist when humility is present. It's paying attention to and thinking about others before you act (or speak). It is being aware of your environment. For example, have you seen people who just can't "read the room" when speaking with someone or in a group? It's like a wealthy person who speaks about their First World problems dealing with their numerous homes when speaking with someone who lives paycheck to paycheck in a small, rented studio apartment. The wealthy person is out of touch with both their "audience" and their environment.

While humility is an internal state of being, it still impacts others. As discussed before, humility allows one to be more open to ideas and experience more personal growth. Receiving other ideas and perspectives can only be a positive experience. Albhy is another interviewee who is extremely humble. As a record producer, he sold over 100 million albums and thirteen number-one singles, all before the age of the internet; Albhy feels that humility teaches him to listen with purpose and intention. In his interview, he shared his belief that others have great insight and deserve our attention, which can teach us a lot. You might not agree with what they say, but you should still listen.

Part of being open-minded to other ideas also means being open-minded to outside criticism. An initial re-action to criticism might be defensiveness, but if you find the criticism valid, accept it, own responsibility for it, and find ways to address it. Even if you don't find it valid, question where it's coming from and why it's a crit-icism. Jeff Bezos said, "If you can't tolerate critics, don't do anything new or interesting." Criticism, when not coming from a place of judgment, gives one an oppor-tunity to learn how to improve. If you receive criticism, it's helpful to consider that someone cares about you enough to talk to you about their concern. Whether you agree with it or not isn't really important. No one likes being criticized, but it is an important tool for self-im-provement. An example would be criticism from a friend commenting about the way you tended to interact with an ex-partner during your relationship. The criticism might seem harsh, but this is a way for your friend to show they care about you and don't want you to make the same mistake again. They want you to have more effective communication skills for your own good. The criticism is a sign of love—coming from a place of caring and kindness.

Humble people do not judge others. Often, when someone judges, they have no idea what's going on in someone else's life or what that person has experienced. You may have had a single interaction with someone who, unbeknownst to you, was having a particularly bad day, and you judged them as being a nasty person when the truth is, they are truly a kind person and well-liked. One of our interviewees, Lin, the author of sixty children's books, was a working woman decades ago when it wasn't common for women to hold jobs outside the home. It was an extremely difficult time for her because she felt judged, alone, and "not accepted" by people who did not fully understand her life circumstances. The judgment from others served no purpose except to hurt her, and it took her a long time to realize that those judgments were more about the people doing the judging than they were about her. Lin realized she didn't have to take it personally since those judgments really had nothing to do with her.

Humility is part of the foundation of spirituality. A humble person acknowledges their physical limitations as a human being and recognizes that God or a higher power is part of the larger metaphysical world. A humble person respects and believes in a higher power and has faith that everything they experience on Earth happens for

> A humble person is not judgmental, nor are they unkind. They also embrace some form of spirituality, respecting that there is a higher power pulling them in the direction they need to go.

a reason, whether they can understand that reason or not. They believe there is a bigger plan that may remain hidden from view.

All of the aspects of humility we have discussed so far lead to a very powerful question: How do you become more humble? It starts with acknowledging that humility is a virtue. Today, this is often difficult to do because glitz and glamour are revered by the internet and the entertainment industry and heavily promoted in social media. It appears that those who are more ostentatious receive a greater number of followers, which many equate with self-worth. Being humble is viewed as weak. In truth, humility dictates that if you are secure in your accomplishments, others don't have to applaud you for them. For example, knowing that you raised a good child, survived tremendous trauma with grace, or surrounded yourself with great people is something you can be personally proud of, and there is no need to have others acknowledge it.

Another practical step to becoming more humble is to give compliments. You will notice that the act of acknowledging someone else will improve your own well-being. It can be as simple as telling someone you like what they're wearing or telling them that you appreciated how kind they were when speaking to your partner. Your words will make them feel pleased and make them feel recognized. This is why there is more reward in giving than in receiving.

David, an interviewee and a retired senior executive for Walt Disney, produced many famous shows, such as the TV show *Thomas & Friends* (following the adventures of a train named Thomas and his train friends). He feels that his greatest accomplishment to date is running his two large nonprofit organizations. One has opened over 250 schools in Africa, and the other has created games and cartoons for thousands of individuals. It was fascinating that he felt it much more important to discuss his work with these two nonprofits than to focus on himself, illustrating how many of our interviewees embodied humility without discussing it directly.

💡 CHAPTER TAKEAWAYS:

- **We need more humility in today's world.**
  Humility is a very important element of wisdom. It is a lost art in today's aggressive and greedy world, and we desperately need more of it. We need to spend more time working to develop it in ourselves and our families. It is the foundation of many of the other themes in this project. Rather than being in constant competition with one another, we should practice letting go of our ego and seeing everybody as an equal. Do not concern yourself about how you stack up to somebody else but rather be secure and confident in what you bring to the table.

- **Humble people are more open to growth and self-development.**

  They exude a sense of kindness, patience, tolerance, and respect toward others. Humble individuals better connect with others, and humble leaders are more successful. Having humility means you understand that you will never be perfect and that there is always something more to learn and improve upon for as long as you live.

- **Being humble will allow you to have deeper relationships.**

  Having humility will allow you the ability to better connect with others. You will be able to establish more meaningful relationships, which will be founded on compassion, empathy, and equality rather than superficiality.

THINGS TO ASK YOURSELF:

• What does humility mean to you? Is it a positive quality or a negative one in your mind?

Date: _____
Answer: _____
_____
_____
_____

Date: _____
Answer: _____
_____
_____
_____

• How open are you to learning from others? Do you always have to be "right"?

Date: _____
Answer: _____
_____
_____
_____

Date: _____

Answer: _____

_____

_____

_____

• What is one example of when you felt your needs
  were more important than someone else's?

Date: _____

Answer: _____

_____

_____

_____

_____

Date: _____

Answer: _____

_____

_____

_____

_____

- Do you think humility is directly connected to self-respect? Why or why not?

  Date: _____
  Answer: _____

  _____

  _____

  _____

  Date: _____
  Answer: _____

  _____

  _____

  _____

- How accurate are you in recognizing your own shortcomings and limitations? What about for others?

  Date: _____
  Answer: _____

  _____

  _____

  _____

Date: _____

Answer: _____

_____

_____

_____

_____

CHAPTER 7

TOLERANCE

Your assumptions are your windows on the world. Scrub them off every once in a while, or the light won't come in.
—Alan Alda

olerance was the sixth element in our study. Similar to humility, it was not discussed directly but became evident through the participant's responses. Tolerance is the ability to keep an open mind and be considerate of different cultures, ideas, and experiences. It

Tolerance is simply this: to have an open mind. It is about being nonjudgmental and unprejudiced in how you approach life and people.

is being nonjudgmental and unprejudiced in how you approach life and people, without assumptions and pre-conceived notions. Many of the themes discussed in this book overlap, and tolerance is no exception, overlapping with kindness, curiosity, and humility.

The definition of tolerance is "the ability or willing-ness to deal with something, in particular the existence of opinions or behavior that one does not necessarily agree with." Tolerance can be applied to various components of life, the most obvious being ideas. When it comes to thoughts and attitudes, being tolerant means being open-minded and actively considering different perspectives. It is being unbiased in one's approach. When cultures embrace diverse points of view, they thrive. Conversely, when they don't, they fail. Human history proves this. From Cyrus II of Persia to Nazi Germany and beyond, intolerance has always led to failure.

While being tolerant should have always been im-portant to people, today being tolerant is recognized as a significant political and social "inalienable right" for those in minority categories. The list of things we need more tolerance for is long (and always growing): race, ethnicity, nationality, sexual orientation, socio-economic status, gender, political ideology, and more. While countries like the United States are working to illuminate and end cases of intolerance, other countries much less tolerant continue to persecute people for being different or even protesting for equality. Like countries, there will always be individuals who will continue to discriminate regardless of their culture's customs or laws. How other people think or behave should not stop you from being yourself or impact how you choose to live your life. While, of course, intolerance should never be acceptable, the best way of stopping intolerance is through political and legal action. If that is not possible, and until that time, "See something, say something" and address the intolerant behavior as it's occurring—but only if it is safe for you to do so. Anyone who has experienced intolerance knows that you can't always change someone's opinion of you, but you can always maintain your sense of self-worth and prove them wrong. As Oprah Winfrey said, "Excellence is the best deterrent to racism and sexism."

While most types of intolerance are recognizable— for example, racism or religious intolerance—there are other forms that are not as obvious. Thinking you are better than someone else because you know more or have more formal education is a form of intolerance. We are all equal, and one person's life experience or education is not more valuable than that of another.

Another important part of tolerance is being open to and considerate of change. People or entities may have said or done something intolerant in the past but now regret those actions. We should never forget these instances of intolerance but rather learn from them. If we learn from these occurrences and use them to guide our decisions and behavior in the future, we can effect real change. Allowing for people or institutions to change lets everyone involved move forward and grow.

Change is one of the natural foundations of life and is what allows for things to grow and evolve. Not everyone is comfortable with change. There are individuals who are creatures of habit and prefer the same routine every day, believing that "routine" equals "security." The challenge with this type of thinking is that, unfortunately, it only leads to rigidity of thought and a lack of personal growth, creating the perfect foundation for intolerance. Such individuals should consider that change can introduce positive, life-changing ideas and wondrous experiences into their lives, expanding their empathy and understanding of new and different things and increasing their tolerance. While the unknown can be terrifying for some, it can also introduce new adventures, even seemingly insignificant ones, that would have otherwise been missed. Have you noticed that many people's best encounters happened by accident? A person "discovered" a coffee shop because they had to take a new route due to road closures, and now the new coffee shop is their favorite coffee shop. Often, the best experiences can happen when you're not looking for them and least expect it. Openness is a key factor.

Any type of problem-solving or scientific inquiry requires tolerance and open-mindedness. People who are most successful at this know that there's more than one way to solve a problem. They may be an expert in their field, but they also know that asking others for their thoughts and ideas will lead to an even better solution than one they would have achieved on their own. For example, a physician may realize that it would only be helpful to the patient if an energy healer was involved in their care. Both providers want the same end goal: healing. Being tolerant and open-minded regarding the ideas of others requires releasing the ego and acknowledging that even disagreeable ideas have some value and may even spark new ideas, ultimately leading to the desired solution.

As stated above, being tolerant of other ideas doesn't mean that you forego your own. It simply means that while you may be passionate about your own perspectives, you are considerate and open to considering those of others. As Timothy Keller said, "Tolerance isn't about not having beliefs. It's about how your beliefs lead you to treat people who disagree with you." It's important that you are respectful of other viewpoints. Having empathy and kindness toward others, and wanting to hear and consider what they have to say, is a way to show respect.

It is interesting to note that tolerance of different ideas has taken a back seat these days. The rise of the internet has allowed for more opinions and greater self-expression, yet it has also allowed for viewpoints to be stifled and for "cancel culture" to take over. Cancel culture is a form of intolerance to differing ideas. The fact that other thoughts and ideas are not tolerated prevents a deeper understanding of the issues at hand. "Canceling" prevents free speech in many instances.

It's not just ideas where we see intolerance. Actions also reflect intolerance. Liz, an interviewee, has a daughter with severe mental health issues and has experienced firsthand actions of intolerance toward both her and her daughter. She recalls a time in her pediatrician's office when a nurse demanded that Liz and her daughter leave the waiting room because her daughter was being too disruptive. Every parent knows, even in the best of circumstances, that children and doctor's offices don't always mix. With her advanced and specialized training, the nurse should have known how to handle a special needs child with more tolerance and compassion. Liz also recalled the many times strangers would treat her and her daughter with intolerance at restaurants, supermarkets, playgrounds, and other public places, making a difficult situation even more difficult. They would judge her parenting skills without understanding how difficult it can be to control the behavior of a child with special needs. Because of these experiences, Liz has learned the importance of showing tolerance toward others without judgment, knowing that she never really knows what's going on in someone else's life or what their situation may be.

Being tolerant has another benefit: It helps maintain and increase self-esteem. You are at peace with yourself and your beliefs. As discussed earlier, when another person's thoughts or opinions ruffle your feathers, have compassion for them for having a closed mind. Their life is most likely much less interesting than yours. Move on. Being offended will get you nowhere except upset.

Tim was born with a dwarfed leg, which often caused him pain. He explained in his interview that the experience taught him to be more tolerant of individuals with disabilities but not to make excuses for them. Despite his physical challenges, he was heavily involved in college sports and pursued a career in theater. The intolerance shown him actually enriched his understanding of tolerance and also taught him that anything was attainable, regardless of circumstances.

You can help promote tolerance in others. First, be receptive to what they have to say. Regardless of what knowledge you have, be respectful and listen to their thoughts. You do not have to agree with them but know that everyone wants to feel heard, so listen to them. Point out information they shared that you think is important to consider. This will strengthen the connection between the two of you. Second, talk to them about the commonalities and the counterarguments and ask them what their thoughts are. Finally, talk about the bigger picture and the ultimate goal. For example, if a friend is closed to understanding individuals who practice a different religion, take that person through the above steps. Focus on the commonalities your friend shares with people of other religions. Realize that a single exercise may not change how she thinks, but it can plant a seed.

In the realm of spirituality, many think that tolerance is a way of being closer to the divine. It's acknowledging that while we all may appear different, we are all more similar than we are different. We are all connected and cut from the same cloth. Most people believe that we were created in God's image, so being intolerant toward someone is being intolerant toward God. If we recognize that we're all connected, then there should be no thoughts of "them vs. us" or thoughts of hate and injustice. Joseph Fort Newton once said, "Men build too many walls and not enough bridges."

Learning to be more tolerant is a trait that we can all adopt. As Henry David Thoreau said, "It is never too late to give up your prejudices." One way to become more tolerant is to listen more to others. Instead of forcing your own thoughts and ideas on others, listen. Try to understand where they are coming from. Another way to increase your tolerance is to catch yourself being judgmental and having intolerant thoughts. Be more self-aware. The minute you dislike something or a person rubs you the wrong way, ask yourself why and work toward changing your thoughts. Is it intolerance, or is there a reason for your dislike or intolerance? Then challenge your own beliefs; remind yourself that assumptions are often incorrect. Finally, be patient with yourself and with others. Building tolerance can take time. For many, the change might happen instantly, but for most of us, it may take time. You likely will not change overnight.

When trying to be more tolerant, the easiest first step is to be more self-aware. Pay attention to your thoughts and reactions to people or situations. If the first thing to pop up is something judgmental, catch it and redirect your thoughts. Ask yourself why you are feeling that way.

Patience can help build tolerance, and this trait was also a significant subtheme of our study. Many interviewees feel that being patient is key to accepting and tolerating others, regardless of who they are and what they believe. This is especially true today as people are quick to judge and dismiss others because of differing social and political views. People also lack patience because of the immediate gratification from receiving instant responses via social media or same-day delivery. The older generation did not have email but used "snail mail." They didn't have cell phones. They used landline telephones. So, our lifestyle and our luxuries actually make us more impatient. A good indicator of our level of impatience is our response to situations like deliveries taking longer than we would like or having to wait in line at the bank or supermarket. Getting annoyed by the delays is a sure sign of impatience and something we need to reflect on and change.

A striking example of developing patience and tolerance was reflected by one of our interviewees. Lynn, whom we heard from in the Spirituality and Positivity chapters, has a son who developed chronic fatigue at age twelve. The experience of watching him struggle, as well as serving as his caretaker, has taught her to be patient. It has taught her to be calm in the center of the storm. Having patience means staying calm despite not knowing what the outcome will be. You've probably heard this before: "This too shall pass." It's having a sense of peace about you, even though you want things to be different. It's not easy, but being patient is a way of honoring yourself. Whatever the situation, you respect yourself enough not to get upset. Like the example we gave about waiting in line, instead of allowing it to upset you, simply think, *Oh, well,* and make an effort to focus your attention on something else. An African proverb says, "The tree of patience has bitter roots, but its fruit is sweet." This has been restated over the years, and now many people recognize the quote as, "Patience is bitter, but its fruit is sweet." It's a reminder that patience is a valuable virtue. It's a recognition that being angry and bitter will not change the outcome. Think about when you're trying to learn a new skill—patience helps you stick with it until you master it. Or perhaps waiting for a job offer—patience will keep you staying hopeful and feeling positive.

Another subtheme of having tolerance is being flexible in any circumstance. (You might remember that being flexible was also a big part of being resilient. Learning to be flexible will benefit your wisdom in more ways than one.) Recognize that things may never be as you expect them to be, but despite that, it's okay. A flexible person adapts to different environments and situations. They adjust to change so that they can succeed in the new situation. A flexible person puts their priorities first and their emotions second. Lynn never expected to have a son with a chronic illness, nor did she expect to be a caregiver in this way to him, but she adapted to her situation, putting her son's needs before her own, and moved forward in her life, accepting her "new normal." Like Lynn, you may not like a particular unexpected situation, but being adaptable will help you through it.

Also, being flexible allows for more emotional growth. Lisa, an entrepreneur, owned a company that failed several years ago. In order to overcome the situation, she immediately realized that she had to be flexible, learn, and move forward. She was not going to allow the situation to dictate her well-being and happiness. As emotionally difficult as it was, being flexible allowed her to view this as a learning opportunity. She believes in being "fiercely flexible," and this experience solidified the importance of flexibility in her life. Debasish Mridha believes the same and says, "The measure of a person's strength is not his muscular power or strength, but it is his flexibility and adaptability."

💡 CHAPTER TAKEAWAYS:

- **Being tolerant means being open-minded and free of assumptions.**

  It is having no prejudices and not being discriminating. It can apply to all parts of life and can be improved the more we recognize our intolerance and work to change those thoughts and actions. It is being open to change.

- **The foundation of tolerance is flexibility and patience.**

  A flexible person will adapt easily to different environments and situations. They are able to adjust to the changes in order to successfully guide themselves to a positive outcome. Recognize that things may never work out as expected, but know that it's okay. Things will happen when they are supposed to and as they are supposed to. "This too shall pass."

- **Increase your tolerance by being more self-aware.**

  If you catch yourself having judgmental thoughts or convincing yourself that you don't like somebody (or something), take a moment to reflect on it. Ask yourself why that person is bothering you and challenge your beliefs. Remind yourself that your assumptions are often incorrect and try to understand where that other person is coming from.

THINGS TO ASK YOURSELF:

- How effectively do you handle a situation where you strongly disagree with someone else's opinion?

Date: _____

Answer: _____

_____

_____

_____

Date: _____

Answer: _____

_____

_____

_____

_____

- Have you ever been able to change a strongly held opinion of yours because you listened and/ or learned from someone else's differing opinion?

Date: _____

Answer: _____

_____

_____

_____

_____

Date: _____

Answer: _____

_____

_____

_____

_____

- Have you ever been a "target" of intolerance? How did you handle it?

Date: _____

Answer: _____

_____

_____

_____

_____

Date: _____

Answer: _____

_____

_____

_____

_____

• What is one thing you know you're intolerant of? Why do you think that is?

Date: _____

Answer: _____

_____

_____

_____

_____

Date: _____

Answer: _____

_____

_____

_____

_____

- Do you think you have to change your opinion or behavior in order to be more tolerant about something?

Date: _____

Answer: _____

_____

_____

_____

_____

Date: _____

Answer: _____

_____

_____

_____

_____

CHAPTER 8

CREATIVITY

The garden of the world has no
limits except in your mind.
—Rumi

Accord ing to our study, creativity is the seventh most important element of wisdom. There are many ways to be creative and discover new ways of thinking or develop a new talent. Brainstorming is one way to get the creative juices flowing. Kicking ideas around with other people can lead to some very creative solutions. Researching a topic can unveil new information that can lead to new thoughts and ideas. Using the magic thought of "What if?" can lead to creative outcomes. Breaking down a process into its separate steps can also help discover a new creative idea. Each of these ways of becoming more creative has something in common: You have to actually *try them.*

The *Oxford Dictionary* describes creativity as "the use of imagination or original ideas, especially in the production of artistic work." Creativity lets us feel magic, see light and positivity in every situation, and think beyond our dreams. An extremely creative person is able to go beyond possibilities

> *Creativity lets us feel magic, see light, and think beyond our wildest dreams. It helps us go beyond all that is possible and achieve exactly what we want in life.*

and transcend ideas. Creativity allows for curiosity and individuality and for thinking outside the box and imagining what *could* be rather than being satisfied with what *is.*

Creativity is often influenced by culture. In cultures that value a collective worldview, creativity revolves around the goal of helping or representing "the many," whereas in cultures that value individuality and entrepreneurship, creativity revolves around the goal of elevating "the individual." For example, fine art reflecting religious beliefs may attempt to help its many viewers see the divine and, thus, life's bigger metaphysical picture, raising a group consciousness above the mundane. Conversely, fine art reflecting the artist's own personal inner life may simply give the artist a "voice" for their inner thoughts and feelings, hoping to connect a single viewer of the artwork to their own inner thoughts and feelings. The goal is to impact the individual and not the collective.

It is not just art that is influenced by this collective-versus-individual cultural perspective. Consider the ancient Greek and Roman aqueducts. Controlling their water supply was a new creative thought in and of itself. Before this invention, people moved to a water source, but then someone had the creative thought of, *Can we move the water source to the people?* That was a big creative thought at that time. The even bigger creative thought was the creation of the aqueducts themselves. Again, creativity for the betterment of the collective.

Now, think about the advent of social media. Individuals are creating songs, clothing styles, and art for the sole purpose of becoming famous. They're not interested in bettering the world for everyone but are simply interested in being recognized and making money purely for reasons of self-interest. Without moral judgment, this, too, is creativity in action.

We humans are all innately creative. Think about children and how much they use their imagination. A bed sheet draped over a couple of dining chairs becomes a tent in the wilderness; a wooden spoon becomes a magic wand; a favorite stuffed animal becomes a best friend and confidante listening to secrets only they can know. As we age, we become more aware of our world and adapt to our environment. We forget how it feels to be as creative as a child, even though we still have that potential. "Real" life just seems to get in the way. Or so we think.

Art is probably the most easily recognizable form of creativity. Michelangelo's *David* or his Sistine Chapel fresco; Andy Warhol's famous *Campbell's Soup Cans*; Vincent van Gogh's *The Starry Night*; your daughter's hand-print candy dish; a birdhouse made of popsicle sticks; a new website design. These are all made manifest through creativity. One doesn't have to be a Michelangelo or Warhol to create art.

Being creative starts with our thoughts. A creative thought first starts by thinking about a basic fundamental issue. This is then expanded upon. This is how the greatest contributions to society were made and continue to this day. Plato, a Greek philosopher, began with thoughts about leadership and was the first to question government and introduce the idea of incorporating wisdom into leadership. Isaac Newton, an English mathematician, developed many theories of motion that Albert Einstein, a German theoretical physicist, developed into his famous theory of relativity. Newton's laws of motion served as the foundation for Einstein to further question the status quo.

Who you are as an individual is creative. How you think and what you do is different than anyone else and thus is special to you. It is creative. There are many instances in which you express your creativity, such as the way you dress, hold yourself, eat, and get around—these are all specific to you. They are your ways of expressing who you are. Your individuality is your signature. There is no one on Earth who is identical to you.

Who you are is creative. Plain and simple. How you think and what you do is completely unique to you and different from anybody else. That alone is creative. Now, you just need to learn how to harness it to express yourself.

Joan is a talent coach and believes in growing human potential and effectiveness. Her creativity has allowed her to open three separate nonprofit agencies geared at improving human potential. Each agency has a different focus and outcome yet incorporates the same ideas of building people up using cutting-edge techniques (like APA Solutions and WomanUp).

Creative thought also allows us to consider a higher power. Creativity allows us to redefine reality and think about a metaphysical realm. This may be the reason creativity has not traditionally received great attention in the scientific world. Mysticism and spirituality are not easy for many to understand or explain because they are based on belief and cannot be measured. They are concepts that aren't concrete and can't be visualized. For this reason, many people would rather not think about them. Without creativity, there would be no science, and without science, we would not have the building blocks for creativity.

Increasing our creativity can be fun—we just have to allow ourselves to let loose of our inner creativity. Take part in one activity per day that's different. Try a new food you've never eaten before, dress in a style of clothing you've never worn before, or meet a new person by starting a conversation with a stranger while in line for coffee. Consider taking on a new hobby. This creative act will foster a sense of freedom and lead to more creativity. It will not only expand your thoughts but remind you of your individuality and feed your soul.

Creativity engages both sides of the brain, ultimately leading to greater flexibility and productivity and allowing us to become more effective in our daily lives. This is especially important for the person with numerous responsibilities, like the single mom with a wage job working hard to maintain a roof over her head and food on the table. This is a person who has no time or energy to commit to a creative act, yet it's crucial that she does. She can start by drawing for five minutes a day before going to bed. The drawing can be anything she wants it to be, but it's her own creation and requires her imagination. It's doing something creative like this that will give her joy and make her feel special. Being creative, even for five minutes, will take her out of feeling the stressors of her life. The key is to start small.

While we're all innately creative, it is often difficult to realize or appreciate that, particularly when we are feeling overwhelmed. As discussed earlier, we all have a *signature* or something that's different about us that expresses our creativity; this is something we can use to help us through difficult times. When we're feeling overwhelmed, this creativity can help increase positive emotions, improve our immune system, and lessen the sense of overwhelm. If you feel like you have a lot on your plate, do something creative to get out of feeling those pressures. It can be as small as journaling or listening to music. This creative act will put you in the driver's seat and remind you that "you got this."

A change can bring a new perspective and new ideas. Many times, a negative situation is what sparks good ideas. The creator of Uber came up with the idea after he had a difficult time hailing a cab. His idea has taken the world by storm, connecting drivers to passengers more efficiently than taxis.

Doing something new is all about the process and not the outcome. It is important not to expect a masterpiece the first time you try a new endeavor, such as painting a watercolor, or perfection when you try to bake your first cake. Have no expectations; just look forward to the process. It's about the journey, not the destination.

The next important way of incorporating creativity is by doing "nothing." This may sound counterintuitive and simple, but it works. Being "bored" is therapeutic both for the mind and body. Great ideas stem from times of nothingness when the brain can breathe and simply take in its surroundings. Sitting at the beach, watching the waves roll in; relaxing on your patio, just looking at the view; going for a long drive with no destination planned . . . these activities allow your thoughts to wander and can spark your creativity.

However, doing "nothing" is increasingly more difficult in an age of constant entertainment and social media. Texting, checking email, talking on the phone, watching videos, playing video games—all create a cacophony difficult to avoid. It's this very electronic/digital frenzy that makes doing nothing more important than ever. Doing "nothing" lets your brain calm down and balance. Similar to sleep, it is essential. There's a reason various world cultures, for centuries, have used the "siesta" as a means of extending the lunch break and incorporating a time of rest.

Many interviewees felt this quiet time was crucial to their daily life. Regardless of what was happening in their lives, they carved out a period during the day where they did nothing. Isabella, whom we met in our Spirituality chapter because she left her high-powered corporate career to have a "Moses experience," feels that during the day, meditation and quiet time are what feed her soul and give her better ideas for her coaching career. It's a time to organize her thoughts and prepare for future obligations. She looks forward to this time and knows it will not only make her a more effective coach but also a calmer person.

A large subtheme of the study was imagination. Whereas creativity is the act of creating something in the real world (or at least based upon the real world), imagination is free from physical constraints. Imagination allows for the idea of cows flying over the moon, cartoon characters coming to life, or little boys and girls becoming princes and princesses. Imagination allows the impossible to become possible—at least in our minds. This ability of imagination can add a touch of the whimsical to our lives and allow us to view the world differently.

Tomas, whom we met in our Kindness chapter, is a successful scientist who loves to imagine daily. He uses his imagination to think of different ways to "create knowledge." By encouraging himself to think unconventionally, imagining helps him design projects and experiments that serve as the foundation of his future work. It starts with an idea.

Imagination is thinking in a limitless fashion and fathoming the unthinkable. Leah, the gerontologist we spoke about in the Positivity chapter, feels that imagination helps you "leave the mundane and think about making the impossible possible." As a professor, she feels it is her responsibility to instill a greater sense of creativity in her students and encourages them to "imagine greatly."

Another subtheme was to be well-rounded in how one lives their life. Being well-rounded is a way to apply creativity to life on a daily basis. By doing different things, wearing different hats, and interacting with different individuals, creativity is incorporated into everything we do. Imagination serves as the engine that ignites the spark, while being well-rounded is a way to manifest the thought into action. Most participants, regardless of their expressed level of creativity, wore different hats. Doing different things was satisfying and allowed them to feel like they were contributing to society in different ways. Every task they completed, or "hat" they wore, fed a different part of their soul. It also validated their feeling of individuality.

Donald is an orthodontist who believes that being an orthodontist does not define him. Seeing patients in the dental office is a small part of who he is. He discussed in his interview how he also enjoys being a magician because it serves as a great ice-breaker, especially with children. In addition, he spends two hours a day learning the details and numerous perspectives on a variety of topics in the news. If, for example, he wants to learn more about an incident that took place in the United States, he approaches each report as if he's an investigator trying to find out details about why it occurred and who was affected. Life has so much to offer, and being creative in one's approach to life only leads to greater depth and meaning.

Interestingly, being well-rounded has become increasingly more difficult to accomplish today. As mankind has advanced, we have also become less flexible. Compare our lives now to that of two hundred years ago. Today, people are defined by a single stereotype, specialty, or other superficial quality. They are firefighters, accountants, doctors, etc., and only those things. Two hundred years ago, people needed to be farmers, ranchers, builders, teachers, weathermen (and women), and a host of other things simultaneously just to survive. Unlike what we see now, most of the interviewees do not live cookie-cutter lives and do not feel like they belong on a hamster wheel. They believe that each day has much to offer. Each moment is different and can lead to more personal growth and a distinct opportunity to contribute to the world.

Harry, another interviewee, is a concert pianist and theoretical physicist who runs a nonprofit that helps people and communities be more prepared for the future. The nonprofit focuses on educating people in need about important issues, teaching them about technology, and introducing them to organizations that can better their lives. He also enjoys playing ice hockey and pool. He never has a typical day and feels that it's the constant variety in his life that keeps his mind open to new thoughts and experiences. Whether it be a conversation with a person waiting in line or a game with a friend, every experience expands his perspective and allows him to think of greater ideas.

⊕ CHAPTER TAKEAWAYS:

- **Creativity is essential to our growth as a people.** It helps us develop, think of, and plan for the future. It can be incorporated into all components of our lives, as we are all creative beings. Participating in a creative act is especially important to people who feel like they don't have time for it. There are many things a person can do to foster creativity, but it starts with the simple step of acknowledging its importance. Regardless of how busy you are, your life needs more creativity.

- **Creativity takes you out of survival mode.** By being creative, you allow your mind to think freely, and you can get into a state of hope, possibility, and positivity. You will develop space for new ideas, and you can promote self-growth and trust in your ideas. You will foster a sense of freedom for yourself, leading to even more creativity and, in turn, more freedom. A win-win!

- **You simply existing is creative.**

  Who you are as an individual is creative. How you think and what you do is different than anyone else and thus is special to you. It is creative. There are many ways in which you express your creativity, such as the way you dress, hold yourself, eat, and get around—these are all specific to you. They are your ways of expressing who you are. Your individuality is your signature. There is no one on Earth who is identical to you.

THINGS TO ASK YOURSELF:

- What does creativity mean to you? What is the most creative thing you have done/thought in the last week?

  Date: _____

  Answer: _____

  _____

  _____

  _____

  _____

152 @ COMMON WISDOM

Date: _____

Answer: _____

_____

_____

_____

_____

• How do you use creativity in your workplace?
  At home?

Date: _____

Answer: _____

_____

_____

_____

_____

Date: _____

Answer: _____

_____

_____

_____

_____

- What is one childlike thing you miss doing as an adult?

  Date: _____
  Answer: _____

  _____

  _____

  _____

  Date: _____
  Answer: _____

  _____

  _____

  _____

- Would you rather spend time being mentally creative or physically creative? Why?

  Date: _____
  Answer: _____

  _____

  _____

  _____

  _____

Date: _____

Answer: _____

_____

_____

_____

_____

• If money and time were not an issue, what creative activity would you like to do that you haven't already done?

Date: _____

Answer: _____

_____

_____

_____

_____

Date: _____

Answer: _____

_____

_____

_____

_____

CHAPTER 9

CURIOSITY

The most beautiful thing we can experience is the mysterious. It is the source of all true art and science.
—Albert Einstein

C uriosity was the eighth and final element of wisdom in our study. Similar to the element of creativity, it was not linked to an individual unless they expressly viewed curiosity as being an important part of their life. Therefore, the number of people in the study who are curious is most likely far higher. Also, similar to creativity, it's a theme that overlaps often with other themes. This stands to reason because, if you think about it, someone who's curious would have to have at least some humility, tolerance, and creativity

155

to be interested in something outside their scope of knowledge, realize they don't know everything about everything, and seek ways of learning about something new, all while keeping an open mind and using their creativity.

The *Oxford Dictionary* defines curiosity as "a strong desire to know or learn something." More knowledge allows us to have more information and, in turn, make better and wiser decisions. Being curious involves asking the five W's: Who, What, When, Where, Why— and a "How" thrown in there for good measure. Once we have a general understanding of a topic, it's common to dig deeper and learn more about it. If, for example, we read about the strengths of an animal, like a lion, for example, we also have a desire to learn about its weaknesses. We discover that although a lion is powerful and has an incredible

Curiosity is all about having a desire to know more, learn more, and use the knowledge to make better and wiser decisions. Being curious means you are always asking the five W's: who, what, when, where, why (and a "how" thrown in for good measure).

sense of smell, it also has poor eyesight and is vulnerable when hunting alone. It's important that we learn these facts from many different sources. The more perspectives we get, the more accurate the information will be. As Mark Twain said, "Whenever you find yourself on the side of the majority, it's time to pause and reflect."

Curiosity is the driving force of wisdom and the seven elements previously discussed. Taking a look at each in order, we begin with "resilience." Without asking yourself *How do I survive and move forward?* you can't have resilience. In order to have kindness, you must ask and answer *Who is this person I'm treating kindly? What is their current circumstance? How can I show them kindness?* Likewise, it would be very difficult to have a positive attitude without curiosity; every obstacle, regardless of how it turns out, is an opportunity to discover something new and exciting, feeding feelings of positivity. The list goes on and on.

Curiosity is what allows for change, growth, and discovery. Many people thought that air travel was impossible for humans until the Wright brothers proved them wrong. Orville and Wilbur had to use their curiosity to discover the secret to flight, asking, *How do birds fly? How can we duplicate that for people? Where should we test our theories?* and more questions. Others were skeptical about the idea of a personal computer until Steve Wozniak and Steve Jobs created the Apple computer. Scientists and engineers could not even fathom the notion of an internet when they sought to connect computer networks to share information. Every discovery and innovation the world has ever known began with curiosity.

Regardless of the level of curiosity, we all possess the innate desire to know more. It may be superficial or a longing to dig deep. A person may just casually wonder about something, while another makes it their life's purpose to ask a question and find the answer. It's the difference between simply taking for granted our existence and searching for the purpose and truth of our existence. Either way, it's a natural reflex. We are born with it. Children love to explore with all their senses. They like to touch and feel textures. They see things and notice phenomena that we may ignore. They are attracted to things that are bright and vivid. They ask many questions. They are innately curious. As adults, we sometimes lose this sense of curiosity because we lack the time or patience to explore. We no longer make time to stop and smell the roses.

Curiosity is an active pursuit that takes effort and concentration. With practice, it eventually develops into an innate reflex that requires you to take action and focus on wondering, questioning, and searching. A lack of curiosity is caused by two factors: Fear and thinking we already know all of the answers. We can probably add laziness into the mix, as well. Ideas and knowledge don't just come knocking on *your* door; you have to actively pursue knocking on *their* doors. That would mean that you don't think you know everything about a particular topic.

One common example of fear stunting curiosity is the fear of doctors. Some people are so fearful of doctors that they will suffer a painful ailment *for years*, losing their quality of life, just because they are afraid of doctors. They are afraid to ask a health professional, "What's wrong?"

At the age of thirteen, Trudi, who was born in a Japanese concentration camp and served as both an arbitrator and professor, was taken by her parents out of school and on a trip around the world. This experience served as the ultimate lesson in curiosity. She explained in her interview that it was during these travels that she learned about different cultures, people, and traditions. This experience taught her to always ask questions. It also taught her to seek out a diversity of perspectives, bringing much more richness to her life. Since that experience, curiosity has been extremely important to her. As Albert Einstein said, "The mind that opens to a new idea never returns to its original size."

Being curious means never taking things at face value. Ask questions about the most obvious, simple, and mundane phenomena. There is no such thing as a "dumb question." Isaac Newton changed the world by asking why something fell, and his work brought into question the laws of gravity that we all thought were facts. It's often the simple questions that have the greatest impact. Who would have thought that a basic aspirin could curb the effects of a heart attack? It took being curious and actively researching this question.

Donald, the orthodontist we met in the prior chapter, spends two hours a day investigating random topics that he hears about in his daily life. His "integrity demands" that he knows the facts. Once he chooses a topic, he investigates it from many different media sources. Like a dog digging for a buried bone, he won't give up until he satisfies his own curiosity. Using multiple sources opens the door to a multitude of perspectives, allowing him to gain a fuller understanding of the topic under exploration. Donald doesn't mind questioning "common knowledge" in his pursuit of the truth.

Being curious and searching for the truth is especially important in this day and age, as there is more information available than ever before. It is critical to remember that just because something is written in a book, magazine, or newspaper does not make it necessarily true. The same applies to the internet. Just because someone posted it on the internet doesn't make it true, either.

Peter, one of our interviewees, has created a website dedicated to replacing the "social media noise" with evidence-based information. His site reports the findings of independent journalists with the goal of exposing inaccuracies presented by the mainstream media. He feels that much of the news is made up, and only some of it is true. That's why he feels that it's critical to only use *reliable sources* with a proven track record in reporting the truth accurately. Stories are often filtered through the lens of the reporter's preconceived notions and life experiences. So, based on who's telling the story, some facts or context may be included and some may be excluded. While most professional journalists work very diligently to report only the facts, there may be unintended gaps in their reporting based on their own intrinsic biases. This is why questioning everything about a news report is essential.

Having curiosity also brings great joy and personal growth. Curiosity fosters adventure and excitement. There's nothing more exhilarating than traveling to a new city and getting "lost" on purpose—by putting the map away and just wandering aimlessly, you can have a local's experience. Finding hidden restaurants or local bakeries that

Curiosity fosters adventure and excitement.

most tourists don't know about only enhances the excitement of traveling to a new place. Following our curiosity can add the pleasure of surprise to our lives.

Curiosity also helps us turn problems into opportunities. One of the most creative examples of this is

Chicago street artist Jim Bachor. Chicago is notorious for its pothole problem, which results in damage to thousands of cars, trucks, and bikes (as well as injuring people) each year. Jim fills in these potholes and covers them with his mosaic tile art, turning a dangerous situation into a beautiful work of art. He knows that they'll only last until paved over, but this doesn't stop him from continuing to turn a dangerous problem into an opportunity to share his art.

Curiosity allows you to be open to new solutions in unfamiliar territories, like Jim, and can turn the mundane into a great new adventure. Having an adventure doesn't always have to be a physical adventure. You can also have an emotional adventure, which can lead to a greater number of positive emotions while decreasing negative emotions like fear and anxiety. For one minute a day, "travel" in your mind to places you only dream of visiting and feel the joy and hope it brings you. Curiosity allows you to leave your comfort zone and take risks, leaving expectations behind.

Fatime, an interviewee, is Middle Eastern, and because of her culture, it was assumed she would marry a Middle Eastern man. Because Fatime was open to new ideas and experiences, she met a real-life cowboy and fell in love—something she would never have experienced if she wasn't open and curious about life outside her own culture. She quickly realized that she had to live her life for herself and not others. She did not want to fulfill a cultural expectation. She was curious about the life she would live "off the grid," away from her family, with the cowboy. Because of her curiosity, she received the happily-ever-after she had always dreamed about. She married the cowboy, had children, and has never looked back. She's happy that she pursued her sense of adventure and wonder instead of following a boring "expected" life. Curiosity allowed her to think outside of the box and bring her dream to life.

While being innately curious is important, being curious about others is a key factor in harmonious relations. It's a quality that overlaps with tolerance. Being curious about others results in better connections and relationships. By being curious, you are more interested and engaged in learning about the other person, and as a result, that person enjoys being around you and is more comfortable opening up about themselves. They feel that they're heard and not judged.

Curiosity is not only important in interpersonal relationships but is also vital to understanding your spiritual
life. Being curious about things we can't see or even
prove exist is how we all begin our spiritual journey. It is
the first step on the path of discovering who we are and
how we fit into the universe. Questioning and seeking
answers about the divine allows us to dig deeper into the
meaning of, and greater purpose of, our own existence. It
also leads to the simple truth—we are all one; we are all
connected; we are all on the same spiritual journey. That
positively impacts and changes how we treat others.

Taking a cue from children, make time to ask the
five W's (and that one H!) when going about your day.
*Who really are the people I work with? What are their
stories? When should I start planning my future? If I'm
able, where should I travel for my next adventure? Why do
I feel stuck in my life? How can I make it better? How do
they send satellites into space?* Become a curious observer,
just like a child, and awareness and wisdom will be your
reward.

The most challenging part of the "curiosity process"
is following up on these new thoughts. Take acting,
for example. Many actors, when asked why they chose

a certain role, have answered, "Because it scared me." They pushed through their fear and allowed their curiosity to win the battle between fear and curiosity. They overcame their fear, and possibly even their arrogance, to learn more about a specific character's inner world, also learning about themselves in the process. The expression "No pain, no gain" certainly applies in regard to curiosity. While it may have killed the cat, curiosity, when used appropriately, can certainly enhance your life and lead you closer to wisdom.

💡 CHAPTER TAKEAWAYS:

- **Curiosity allows for change and growth.**
  Curiosity is an innate quality that we all possess. It is rooted in asking questions and learning more about a topic. It is a way of being open-minded, accepting, and impartial. It brings happiness and excitement to life. It requires that a person ignite a fire and wonder. It starts with one's own thoughts and can be a model for others. Although it's the final theme in our Wisdom

Research Project, in many ways it is essential for all the other themes to exist.

- **By being curious, you will be open to new experiences and unfamiliar territories.**
  This can be something physical, like a trip to a new country, or something emotional, like tackling your anxiety. Curiosity promotes adventure and excitement, and the payoff is a life full of joy, personal growth, and the openness to take risks.

- **Curiosity is vital to connecting you to your spiritual life.**
  When we are curious about things we can not see or even prove exist, we are showing that we are open to learning more about spirituality and exploring a higher power. Seeking out answers about the divine gives us an understanding of our own purpose as well as the purpose of those around us. Eventually, we will understand that we are all connected, and from that comes the desire to treat everybody with the same kindness.

THINGS TO ASK YOURSELF:

- Are you interested in how others think or how things are made or work? Why or why not?

  Date: _____
  Answer: _____
  _____
  _____
  _____

  Date: _____
  Answer: _____
  _____
  _____
  _____

- In what instance did you actively search for an answer to a question that you didn't really need to?

  Date: _____
  Answer: _____
  _____
  _____
  _____

Date: _____

Answer: _____

_____

_____

_____

_____

• Do you tend to accept things at face value, or do
  you "hunt for the truth"?

Date: _____

Answer: _____

_____

_____

_____

_____

Date: _____

Answer: _____

_____

_____

_____

_____

- What is your favorite question: Who? What? When? Where? Why? Or How? And why is it your favorite?

  Date: _____

  Answer: _____

  _____

  _____

  _____

  Date: _____

  Answer: _____

  _____

  _____

  _____

- What is something you've always wondered about but never bothered to pursue?

  Date: _____

  Answer: _____

  _____

  _____

  _____

Date: _____

Answer: _____

_____

_____

_____

_____

CHAPTER 10

FINAL THOUGHTS

W e asked these two questions at the beginning of the book:

1. **What is wisdom?**
2. **Can it be scientifically defined?**

Let's start with the second question first. Using the six steps of the scientific method, we determined that we *could* define wisdom scientifically. Even though our sample size was sixty people, we feel confident that had the sample size been 600, we *still* would have ended up with the same eight elements in defining wisdom. These elements seem to be universal among all of our diverse Wisdom Research Project participants, and we feel confident that universality would continue in any culture and with an infinite number of participants.

Now, to the first question: What is wisdom? Hopefully, after reading this book, you are closer to defining what wisdom is for yourself. There are elements that may be your strengths and some that may need more work. The entire purpose of becoming wise must be specific to you. These eight elements and the variety of sub-elements we've discussed will help you find balance in your life. Incorporating them will enrich your life in ways you might not even have imagined. They will give your life more meaning and a greater purpose. Whether we realize it or not, that is what we all want in life: to be happier and have more balance, meaning, and purpose. We get there by embodying these eight elements with sincerity and honesty.

Knowing the eight elements of wisdom is not enough. *Using* them and *integrating* them into your daily life is where the magic happens. That may sound simple, but according to our participants, it's not always easy. It's a process. Fake it 'til you make it. You can be book-smart, but not wise. You need to apply that knowledge, think about those facts and concepts, and apply them to your life in order to transform knowledge into wisdom. So, too, should you learn what these eight elements mean (the book-smart part) and then actively apply those elements to yourself and your life (the wisdom part).

Integrate them into your daily routines and interactions with yourself, as well as others. Working to understand how each of these eight elements is interrelated will lead you to profound and life-changing insight and inspiration. People don't live in a vacuum and neither do these elements; they are dynamic, evolving, and

Time to put the eight traits of wisdom into effect. Spread kindness, positivity, tolerance, and creativity. Demonstrate resilience, curiosity, humility, and spirituality. The point is not to be perfect at them but rather work at them every single day in order to lead a more meaningful and fulfilling life.

interconnected. By working to see their interconnectedness, we become closer to wisdom.

With knowledge comes responsibility. Now that you know these eight elements of wisdom, you have a responsibility to yourself and to your community to embody these elements to the very best of your ability.

Spread kindness, positivity, tolerance, and creativity. Demonstrate resilience, curiosity, humility, and spirituality. No one is perfect, and as stated above, this is a process, but striving to better understand and incorporate these eight elements into your life is important. It's not all or nothing. It takes time and practice. As we said in the first chapter, only one person in our study embodied all eight elements. It's like running up a tall sand dune: you might slide backward under the shifting sand sometimes, but eventually you will reach the top.

Hopefully, this book has given you food for thought on identifying ways to improve your understanding and abilities relating to these eight elements. We have defined the elements, shown you ways to consider each of them via the questions at the end of each chapter, and given you a start on understanding their interconnectedness.

Your search for wisdom is just the beginning of a journey to a better life. Incorporating these elements will take time and patience. Be persistent and don't give up. Believe in yourself. Know that the reward is worth the struggle. More meaning and depth await you.

ABOUT THE AUTHOR

D r. Laura Gabayan is a world-renowned physician and researcher who lives in Los Angeles. She attended UCLA for her undergraduate studies, medical school, residency training, and additional training in research. She has published extensively in academic journals, obtained a large number of prestigious grants and awards, and served as a revered reviewer for numerous impactful scientific journals.

In *Common Wisdom*, she describes the findings of The Wisdom Research Project, an endeavor committed to defining wisdom scientifically.

ACKNOWLEDGMENTS

I t really took a village to make this happen. A big heartfelt thank you to everyone involved. I will never forget your commitment and dedication to doing quality work. I am very lucky to have had you be a part of this.

My first thank you goes to Carolina Zimmer and Caitlin Andrews. Without you, there would be no Wisdom Research Project and none of this would have happened.

My next thank you goes to Joe Marich of Marich Media. You are smart, hard-working, and committed to doing a phenomenal job. Thank you for serving as both my editor and my publicist. I can't talk about this book happening without talking about Liz Dubelman and her company, VidLit. You really were my everything.

Thank you for serving as my guardian angel throughout this journey.

Another big thank you to Jesse Kanner with Calibrate Studio. You connected me to the world and helped spread my message.

Finally, of course, this book would not have been published without Sara Stratton with Redwood Publishing. There is a reason why you have such a great reputation. Thank you for being so patient with me.

CONTACT LAURA

- For media inquiries, email media@lauragabayan.com.
- For other engagements or inquiries involving Dr. Laura Gabayan, email inquire@lauragabayan.com.
- For questions/comments about the project or book, email contact@lauragabayan.com.

www.lauragabayan.com

Made in the USA
Monee, IL
04 August 2024